CELEBRATE RECOVERY

LEADER'S GUIDE

Rick Warren is Senior Pastor of Saddleback Church in Mission Viejo, California *(www.saddleback.com)*, a church that began in 1980 and has grown to a weekly attendance of over 14,000 people. He is the author of the Gold Medallion best-seller, *The Purpose-Driven™ Church,* as well as *Answers to Life's Difficult Questions, The Power to Change Your Life,* and *Dynamic Bible Study Methods.*

John Baker developed the Celebrate Recovery ministry at Saddleback Church in 1991. He is currently serving as pastor of ministries, overseeing the entire C.L.A.S.S. 301 process, staffing the over 150 ministries, and helping start new ministries. In addition, he oversaw the development and implementation of Saddleback's outstanding lay counseling program.

CELEBRATE RECOVERY

LEADER'S GUIDE

A recovery program based on eight

principles from the Beatitudes

JOHN BAKER
Foreword by Rick Warren

ZondervanPublishingHouse

Grand Rapids, Michigan

A Division of HarperCollinsPublishers

AUTHOR'S NOTE:

Because I have picked up a variety of quotes and slogans from numerous recovery meetings, tapes, and seminars, I have not been able to provide some sources for all of the material here. If you feel that I have quoted your material, please let me know and I will be pleased to give you the credit.

Celebrate Recovery Leader's Guide
Copyright © 1998 by John Baker

Requests for information should be addressed to:

ZondervanPublishingHouse
Grand Rapids, Michigan 49530

ISBN: 0-310-22108-0

Interior design by Sue Vandenberg Koppenol

Printed in the United States of America

03 04 /❖ ML/ 10

This book is dedicated to my Lord and Savior, Jesus Christ.

To my wife, Cheryl, and my children, Laura and Johnny, for loving me no matter what.

To Pastors Rick Warren and Glen Kreun, for trusting and believing in me.

To the Saddleback Church staff, for their support.

To the thousands of courageous men and women who have celebrated their recoveries with me over the last six years!

Contents

Principle 1: Realize I'm not God. I admit that I am powerless to control my tendency to do the wrong thing and my life is unmanageable.

"Happy are those who know they are spiritually poor."

Principle 2: Earnestly believe that God exists, that I matter to Him, and that He has the power to help me recover.

"Happy are those who mourn."

Principle 3: Consciously choose to commit all my life and will to Christ's care and control.

"Happy are the meek."

Principle 4: Openly examine and confess my faults to myself, to God, and to someone I trust.

"Happy are the pure in heart."

Principle 5: Voluntarily submit to every change God wants to make in my life and humbly ask Him to remove my character defects.

"Happy are those whose greatest desire is to do what God requires."

Principle 6: Evaluate all my relationships. Offer forgiveness to those who have hurt me and make amends for harm I've done to others, except when to do so would harm them or others.

"Happy are the merciful." "Happy are the peacemakers."

Principle 7: Reserve a daily time with God for self-examination, Bible reading, and prayer in order to know God and His will for my life and to gain the power to follow His will.

Principle 8: Yield myself to God to be used to bring this Good News to others, both by my example and my words.

"Happy are those who are persecuted because they do what God requires."

the problem. When we stop hiding our own faults and stop hurling accusations at others, then the healing power of Christ can begin working in our mind, will, and emotions.

4. *Celebrate Recovery emphasizes spiritual commitment to Jesus Christ.* The third principle calls for people to make a total surrender of their lives to Christ. Lasting recovery cannot happen without this step. Everybody needs Jesus. Celebrate Recovery is thoroughly evangelistic in nature. In fact, the first time I took our entire church through this program, over 500 people prayed to receive Christ on a single weekend. It was an amazing spiritual harvest. And during the ten-week series that I preached to kick off this program, our attendance grew by over 1,500! Don't be surprised if this program becomes the most effective outreach ministry in your church. Today, nearly seventy-three percent of the people who've been through Celebrate Recovery have come from outside our church. Changed lives always attract others who want to be changed.

5. *Celebrate Recovery utilizes the biblical truth that we need each other in order to grow spiritually and emotionally.* It is built around small group interaction and the fellowship of a caring community. There are many therapies, growth programs, and counselors today that operate around one-to-one interaction. But Celebrate Recovery is built on the New Testament principle that we don't get well by ourselves. We need each other. Fellowship and accountability are two important components of spiritual growth. If your church is interested in starting small groups, this is a great way to get started.

6. *Celebrate Recovery addresses all types of habits, hurts, and hang-ups.* Some recovery programs deal only with alcohol or drugs or another single problem. But Celebrate Recovery is a "large umbrella" program under which a limitless number of issues can be dealt with. At Saddleback Church, only one out of three who attend Celebrate Recovery are dealing with alcohol or drugs. We have several other specialized groups too.

7. *Finally, Celebrate Recovery produces lay ministers.* Because it is biblical and church-based, Celebrate Recovery produces a continuous stream of people moving into ministry after they've found recovery in Christ. Eighty-five percent of the people who've gone through the program are now active members of Saddleback Church, and an amazing forty-two percent are now using their gifts and talents serving the Lord in some capacity in our church.

In closing, let me say that the size of your church is no barrier to beginning a Celebrate Recovery ministry. You can start it with just a small group of people and watch it grow by word of mouth. You won't be able to keep it a secret for long!

I'm excited that you have decided to begin a Celebrate Recovery ministry in your church. You are going to see lives changed in dramatic ways. You are going to see hopeless marriages restored and people set free from all kinds of sinful habits, hang-ups, and hurts as they allow Jesus to be Lord in every area of their lives. To God be the glory! We'll be praying for you.

Dr. Rick Warren
Senior Pastor,
Saddleback Valley Community Church

From My Heart to Yours

My name is John Baker, and I have the privilege of serving Jesus Christ at Saddleback Church as the Pastor of Ministry. I joined Saddleback's staff five years ago as the Pastor of Recovery and Small Groups. Two years ago, I was asked to serve as one of the seven elder pastors and oversee the over 150 different ministries at Saddleback. That's what John Baker *does*.

As a way of introducing who John Baker *is*, I would like to share my testimony by relating my experiences, strengths, and hopes as I have traveled my personal "road to recovery."

I was raised in a Christian home in the Midwestern town of Collinsville, Illinois, population 10,000. I had a so-called "normal" childhood, whatever that is. My parents were members of a small Baptist church pastored by a very young Gordon MacDonald. I asked Christ into my heart at age thirteen. In high school I was class president and lettered in basketball, baseball, and track. I felt called into ministry at age sixteen and applied to several Christian universities. Up to this point, everything sounds normal—almost boring.

But I had a problem: I had to be the best in everything. Deep down inside I never felt good enough for my parents, my teammates, my girlfriends, or anyone. If I wasn't good enough for them, I wondered how I could ever be good enough for God. I must have missed the Sunday sermons on God's mercy and Jesus' unconditional love and undeserved and unearnable grace. I was a walking, talking paradox—a combination of the lowest possible self-esteem and the world's largest ego. Believe me, that's not a very comfortable feeling inside. The best way that I can describe the feeling is a burning emptiness—a hole—right in the gut.

I wrestled with God's call and judged myself unworthy to enter the ministry. Instead, after high school I went to the University of Missouri. When I packed for my freshman year, I took my nonexistent self-esteem with me. I joined a fraternity and soon discovered the solution—or what I believed to be the solution—for my life's pain: alcohol. It worked! I fit in! For the first time in my life I felt like I belonged.

While attending the university as a business administration major (with a minor in partying), I met my wife, Cheryl. We were married my senior year. Because the Vietnam war was in full swing, we knew that after college I would be called into the service. Little did Cheryl know what else the next nineteen years would have in store.

In 1970 I graduated from college, joined the Air Force, and was chosen to be a pilot. I attended Officers' Training School, and in ninety days learned to act like an officer and drink like a gentleman. I continued to abuse alcohol, viewing it as a cure for my pain, certainly not a sin!

In the service, I quickly found the proper use for one hundred percent oxygen—a cure for hangovers! The service is a great place to discover one's talents. Soon I was selected as my squadron's social officer. Perfect! A job that required a lot of hours planning functions at the officers' club bar. Then the war ended and I was assigned to a reserve unit.

After the service I joined Scott Paper Company. I earned my MBA degree at night school and God gave us our first child, a daughter, Laura. Two years later we were blessed with our son, John Jr.

I was promoted eight times in the first eleven years of my business career. I was the vice president of sales and marketing for two large consumer food manufacturers.

I had reached all my life's career and financial objectives and goals by the time I was thirty! Along with all this business success, however, came several relocations. Moving every two years made it difficult for us to establish a home church, but as my drinking continued, that became less and less important to me. I knew that if I died I was saved, but my Christianity was not reflected in my lifestyle, business practices, and priorities.

Still, I thought my life appeared normal to casual observers. I was a leader in my church's Awana ministry for youth. I thought nothing of leaving work early to stop by a bar before the Wednesday night meeting so I could relax and relate better to the kids. Didn't everybody do that? I was also my son's Little League coach for five years, but I always stopped by the pizza joint with my assistant coach for a few pitchers of beer after every game. Again, didn't everybody? Talk about insanity!

Slowly I became more and more uncomfortable with the lifestyle I was leading. I faced a major decision. I had a choice: do it my way—continue drinking and living by the world's standards—or surrender, repent, and do it God's way. I wish I could tell you that I saw the light and did it God's way, but the truth is, I chose my way. My drinking increased and I turned my back on God. Proverbs 14:12 (TLB) says, "Before every man there lies a wide and pleasant road that seems right but ends in death."

I was what is known as a functioning alcoholic. I never lost a job, never got arrested for drunk driving. No, the only thing I lost was my close relationship with the Lord (my sins separated me from Him) and my family (Cheryl and I were separated) and all purpose for living. You see, what I had considered the solution for my life's problem, alcohol, *became* the problem!

My life was out of control. I had created my own hell on earth! On an October morning, I was in Salt Lake City on a business trip when I woke up and knew I couldn't take another drink. But I also knew that I couldn't live without one! I had finally hit my bottom. I was dying physically, emotionally, mentally, and most important, spiritually. I was at **Principle 1.** [1]

Principle 1. Realize I'm not God. I admit that I am powerless to control my tendency to do the wrong thing and that my life is unmanageable.
"Happy are those who know they are spiritually poor."

Step 1. We admitted we were powerless over our addictions and compulsive behaviors, that our lives have become unmanageable.
"I know that nothing good lives in me, that is, in my sinful nature. For I have the desire to do what is good, but I cannot carry it out" (Romans 7:18).

God has never kept me from making a mistake. He's a gentleman. He doesn't intrude. He loves me enough to allow me to make my own decisions and mistakes, knowing that when I ran out of my own resources, I would come back to Him as He had planned all along.

When I got back home, I went to my first AA meeting. But that was only the beginning. All in all, I went to over ninety meetings in ninety days. As time passed, I acknowledged **Principle 2.**

[1]Throughout this material, you will notice several references to the Christ-centered 12 Steps. Our prayer is that Celebrate Recovery will create a bridge to the millions of people who are familiar with the secular 12 Steps and in so doing, introduce them to the one and only true Higher Power, Jesus Christ. Once they begin that relationship, ask Christ into their hearts as Lord and Savior, true healing and recovery can begin!

Principle 2. Earnestly believe that God exists, that I matter to Him, and that He has the power to help me recover.
"Happy are those who mourn, for they shall be comforted."

Step 2. We came to believe that a power greater than ourselves could restore us to sanity.
"For it is God who works in you to will and to act according to his good purpose" (Philippians 2:13).

This is where I found my first glimmer of hope! God loves me unconditionally. I was finally able to understand Romans 11:36 (TLB): "Everything comes from God alone. Everything lives by His power."

Today my life with Christ is an endless hope: my life without Him was a hopeless end! My own willpower left me empty and broken, so I changed my definition of willpower. Now I know that true willpower is the willingness to accept God's power for my life.

This led me to **Principle 3**.

Principle 3. Consciously choose to commit all my life and will to Christ's care and control.
"Happy are the meek."

Step 3. We made a decision to turn our lives and our wills over to the care of God.
"Therefore, I urge you, brothers, in view of God's mercy, to offer your bodies as living sacrifices, holy and pleasing to God—this is your spiritual act of worship" (Romans 12:1).

In working the first three principles I said, "I can't, God can," and I decided to let Him. One day at a time. If we don't surrender to Christ, we will surrender to chaos!

I thought the first three principles were hard, but now came **Principle 4**.

Principle 4. Openly examine and confess my faults to myself, to God, and to someone I trust.
"Happy are the pure in heart."

Step 4. We made a searching and fearless moral inventory of ourselves.
"Let us examine our ways and test them, and let us return to the LORD" (Lamentations 3:40).

Step 5. We admitted to God, to ourselves, and to another human being the exact nature of our wrongs.
"Therefore confess your sins to each other and pray for each other so that you may be healed" (James 5:16).

At this point I had to go back to visit the young John Baker, to face the hurts, hangups, and habits I had attempted to drown with alcohol. I had to face the loss of my infant brother. I saw my part in all the destruction that my alcoholism had caused to all those who were once close to me. After I "'fessed up" I was able to face the truth and accept Jesus' forgiveness and healing, which led me out of the darkness of my secrets and into His wonderful light!

I thank God for providing me with a sponsor who helped me stay balanced and didn't judge me during the sharing of my inventory. I cannot begin to tell you the burden God lifted off me when I completed the instructions found in James 5:16! I now knew I was forgiven by the work of Jesus Christ—the one and only true Higher Power—on the cross and that all the sins and wrongs of my past were no longer a secret. Now I was finally willing to have God change me. I was ready to submit to any and all changes God wanted me to make in my life.

Principle 5 made me realize that it was time to "let go and let God." By this time, I was happy to do so! I had seen enough of myself to know that I was incapable of changing my life on my own.

Principle 5. Voluntarily submit to every change God wants to make in my life and humbly ask Him to remove my character defects.
"Happy are those whose greatest desire is to do what God requires."

Step 6. We were entirely ready to have God remove all these defects of character.
"Humble yourselves before the Lord, and he will lift you up" (James 4:10).
Step 7. We humbly asked Him to remove all our shortcomings.
"If we confess our sins, he is faithful and just and will forgive us our sins and purify us from all unrighteousness" (1 John 1:9).

For me, completing Principle 5 meant three things: (1) I allowed God to transform my mind—its nature, its condition, its identity; (2) I learned to rejoice in steady progress—patient improvement that allowed others to see the changes in me that I could not see; (3) God rebuilt my self-worth based on His love for me rather than the world's standards.

During this time God gave me His definition of humility: "My grace is all you need, for my power is greatest when you are weak" (2 Corinthians 12:9). Then I could say with the apostle Paul, "I am most happy, then, to be proud of my weaknesses.... For when I am weak then I am strong" (vv. 9–10).

I was now ready to work on **Principle 6**, my favorite:

Principle 6. Evaluate all my relationships. Offer forgiveness to those who have hurt me and make amends for harm I've done to others, except when to do so would harm them or others.
"Happy are the merciful" and *"Happy are the peacemakers."*

Step 8. We made a list of all persons we had harmed and became willing to make amends to them all.
"Do to others as you would have them do to you" (Luke 6:31).
Step 9. We made direct amends to such people whenever possible, except when to do so would injure them or others.
"Therefore, if you are offering your gift at the altar and there remember that your brother has something against you, leave your gift in front of the altar. First go and be reconciled to your brother; then come and offer your gift" (Matthew 5:23–24).

I said this is my *favorite* principle, not the easiest! I had quite a list of names on my amends list. They ranged from former employers and employees to friends and neighbors. But my most special amends were to my family, especially to my wife, Cheryl. We were still separated. I told her that I was truly sorry for the pain I had caused in her life, that I still loved her, and that if I could ever do anything for her—anything—she only had to ask.

Over the months of separation, Cheryl had seen the changes God was making in my life, changes that occurred as I worked my program. (This is where it really gets interesting!) She and the kids had started attending a church that met in a gym. It was called Saddleback. One Saturday night I was visiting the kids and they asked me to join them on Sunday morning. Much to their surprise, I said yes! It had been five years since I had last attended a church service, but when I heard the music and Pastor Rick Warren's message, I knew I was home. Cheryl and I began to work in earnest on our problems and five months later, God opened our hearts and we renewed our marriage vows. Isn't that just like God!

As a family we were baptized and later took all the church's classes: 101 Membership, 201 Maturity, and 301 Ministry. There I found one of my life's verses:

> You have been chosen by God himself—you are priests of the King, . . . you are God's very own—all this so you may show to others how God called you out of the darkness into his wonderful light. Once you were less than nothing; now you are God's own. *(1 Peter 2:9–10)*

As Pastor Rick Warren says, "God never wastes a hurt." All the pain and heartache of my addiction finally made sense! God gave me the vision of Celebrate Recovery, a Christ-centered recovery program. And praise God, I finally was able to accept God's call. I entered Golden Gate Baptist Seminary and committed my life to God, to serve Him wherever and whenever He chose.

I have dedicated my life to serving Jesus Christ. I intend to work the last two principles on a daily basis for the remainder of my time on this earth.

> Principle 7. Reserve a daily time with God for self-examination, Bible reading, and prayer in order to know God and His will for my life and to gain the power to follow His will.
> Principle 8. Yield myself to God to be used to bring this Good News to others, by both my example and my words.
> *"Happy are those who are persecuted because they do what God requires."*

> Step 10. We continued to take personal inventory and when we were wrong, promptly admitted it.
> *"So, if you think you are standing firm, be careful that you don't fall!"* (1 Corinthians 10:12).
> Step 11. We sought through prayer and meditation to improve our conscious contact with God, praying only for knowledge of His will for us and power to carry that out.
> *"Let the word of Christ dwell in you richly"* (Colossians 3:16).
> Step 12. Having had a spiritual experience as the result of these steps, we try to carry this message to others and to practice these principles in all our affairs.
> *"Brothers, if someone is caught in a sin, you who are spiritual should restore him gently. But watch yourself, or you also may be tempted"* (Galatians 6:1).

God has blessed me richly, and I gratefully pass on these blessings to you. It is my prayer that this book will help your church start a recovery program where your people can safely work together on their hurts, hang-ups, and habits—a program where Christ's love, truth, grace, and forgiveness are demonstrated in all things.

Introduction

I. Ninety-Day Kickoff Strategy

II. Seven Keys to Start Your Recovery Ministry and Keep It Growing

III. Meeting Formats and Materials

The purpose of Celebrate Recovery is to encourage fellowship and to celebrate God's healing power in our lives as we work our way along the road to recovery. We are changed as we share our experiences, strengths, and hopes with one another. In addition, we become willing to accept God's grace and forgiveness in solving our life's problems.

By working through the principles, we grow spiritually, and we are freed from our hurts, hang-ups, and habits. This freedom creates peace, serenity, joy, and most important, a stronger personal relationship with others and our personal, loving, and forgiving Higher Power, Jesus Christ.

Celebrate Recovery is now in its seventh year at Saddleback Church, Mission Viejo, California. The program not only has survived, but has been truly blessed and continues to grow beyond my greatest expectations. Over 2,500 courageous individuals have worked through their hurts, hang-ups, and habits at Saddleback Church since the ministry began in 1991.

In those six years, we have tried a variety of new ideas and concepts to help the ministry grow. Of course, everything we tried didn't work, but from the very beginning, I told the leadership team that the only thing we could not change in Celebrate Recovery is the truth that Jesus Christ is the one and only Higher Power. Other than that, every part of Celebrate Recovery—format, meeting agendas, group discussion, rules—could and should always be evaluated and changed for improvement and growth.

This leader's guide is a compilation of what has worked at Saddleback. As you read through the book, you will see that in later chapters every aspect of Celebrate Recovery is explained in detail. This introduction, however, is provided to get you started. The ninety-day kickoff strategy will help you organize your church's Celebrate Recovery ministry. The seven keys will show you how Saddleback's Celebrate Recovery grew from forty-five people in 1991 to over four hundred members today. And last, the meeting format and materials list will give you a blueprint from which to plan a year of recovery meetings.

I. Ninety-Day Kickoff Strategy

Days 1–30

1. PRAY! "Pray continually" (1 Thessalonians 5:17).

2. Using pulpit announcements and bulletin inserts, inform the church that a Christ-centered recovery program is going to begin within the next few months. Ask for individuals with twelve-step experience to pray if God is calling them to be a part of this new ministry.

> Pray in the Spirit at all times with all kinds of prayers, asking for everything you need. To do this you must always be ready and never give up. Always pray for all God's people. *(Ephesians 6:18 NCV)*

3. Read the leader's guide and participant's guides so that you become knowledgeable and comfortable with the program.

> This is my prayer for you: that your love will grow more and more; that you will have knowledge and understanding with your love. *(Philippians 1:9 NCV)*

4. Order Celebrate Recovery curriculum for your new leadership team. (The leaders will be recruited and selected in a month or two.)

Days 31–60

1. Recruit and interview potential leaders.

2. Determine meeting night and location for the Celebrate Recovery program.

3. Have prospective leaders read the Celebrate Recovery curriculum.

4. Plan for initial recovery groups. I suggest that you begin with no more than four groups: Men's Chemically Dependent, Women's Chemically Dependent, Men's Codependent, and Women's Codependent.

Days 61–90

1. Meet weekly with your new leadership team. Work through the first participant's guide, *Stepping Out of Denial Into God's Grace*, together.

2. Announce to the church Celebrate Recovery's kickoff date.

3. Put information about the different groups in the church bulletin and/or set up an information table at church services.

4. Use pulpit announcements to show the senior pastor's support and approval of the program. This will let everyone know that your church is a "safe" place to deal with their hurts, hang-ups, and habits.

5. Order the Celebrate Recovery curriculum for participants at least three weeks prior to your first meeting.

6. Have Celebrate Recovery leaders give a five- to eight-minute testimony in regular church services, and have them personally invite others to the first meeting.

> He comforts us every time we have trouble, so when others have trouble, we can comfort them with the same comfort God gives us. *(2 Corinthians 1:4 NCV)*

7. Inform local Christian therapists and use local newspapers to invite the community to attend the program.

8. PRAY! "Pray continually" (1 Thessalonians 5:17).

NOTE: The fourth month of Celebrate Recovery is an excellent time to begin taking the entire church through Pastor Rick Warren's eight-week "Road to Recovery" series.

II. Seven Keys to Start Your Recovery Ministry and Keep It Growing

There are seven keys to starting a recovery ministry and keeping it growing: (1) worship, (2) leadership training, (3) senior pastor support, (4) fellowship events, (5) curriculum, (6) new groups, and (7) outreach. Let's begin with what I believe to be the most important key to continued growth in any recovery program: worship.

Worship

Worship has been a central part of Celebrate Recovery since the very first meeting. Every Friday night we begin our large group time with twenty minutes of praise and worship. I believe our worship time is important for the following reasons:

- Worship is a major strength and difference between a Christ-centered and a secular recovery program.

> And you will sing as on the night you celebrate a holy festival; your hearts will rejoice as when people go up with flutes to the mountain of the LORD, to the Rock of Israel. *(Isaiah 30:29)*

- Worship provides a time for everyone to put aside the busyness and hassles of the world and get in touch with the true Higher Power, Jesus Christ. It allows time for the power of the Holy Spirit to fill all those who attend with a peace and a safety that only He can provide. There will be people there who are hurting so badly that they may be able to express their pain only through silent prayer and worship.
- Worship gives us a vehicle in which to celebrate our recoveries! I suggest keeping the praise songs upbeat to build up, strengthen, and encourage those who attend, and to focus on the joy of God's presence, peace, and power in their recoveries.

I wish everyone could attend Celebrate Recovery at Saddleback Church! You would see firsthand the power of worship in recovery; we have twenty-plus singers and musicians who minister faithfully to others weekly. It doesn't matter, though, if your recovery ministry is small; a twenty-piece band is not necessary to incorporate worship into your recovery program. When we started Celebrate Recovery in 1991, we had two singers and a three-piece band. Even if you use a tape or CD, or simply find someone who can lead while playing a guitar, just be sure to include worship as a key part of your recovery program.

Leadership Training

The second key to growing your recovery ministry is leadership training. Proverbs 23:12 says, "Apply your heart to instruction and your ears to words of knowledge." Pastor Rick Warren has told the Saddleback Church staff over and over, "Once you stop learning, you stop leading."

If I had to choose one word that would describe the leadership training at Celebrate Recovery, it would be *consistent*. We schedule monthly meetings to discuss recovery issues and group dynamics. These leadership meetings include four elements: planning, teaching, sharing, and fellowship time.

Planning time includes assigning the lessons that the teaching team will be teaching for the next month. At this time we also line up the testimonies that will be used to support the particular principle we are working on that month.

In addition, assignments for the Celebrate Recovery Information Table, Solid Rock Cafe, Bar-B-Que, and other special events are given out at this time. In this planning element of the meeting, group participation is essential.

Teaching time is also very important. We currently have three Christian counselors who have volunteered their time and support to help instruct and support our leaders. They have taught on a variety of topics from "how to handle someone in your group who is suicidal" to "helping the parents in your groups get needed help for their children."

During *sharing time* I encourage the leaders to break into small groups. This gives them an opportunity to share different ideas for handling a conflict in their group, enforcing the rules, or any general tip or strategy that has worked in their group. They also share their experiences, strengths, hopes, and especially their struggles with one another.[1]

We use the *fellowship time* in our leadership meetings to celebrate the Lord's Supper. This is a great time to share what Christ has done in each of our lives and to bond us as a ministry team in purpose and spirit. The meeting concludes with a light dinner or an old-fashioned potluck. Sometimes we include spouses and families.

The leaders sign an annual leadership covenant (see Appendix A) and they also must meet the following qualifications:

1. They must be a growing Christian, not a new believer.
2. They must have completed all levels of Saddleback's Christian Life and Service Seminars.
3. They must sign and agree to follow Saddleback's Staff Standards (see Appendix B).
4. They need to have worked hard on their own recovery and be able to talk comfortably about their own victories and struggles.
5. They need to have a strong personal support network: family, recovering friends, accountability partners, church leaders, Christian counselor, and so forth.
6. They must agree to attend ongoing monthly leadership training sessions.
7. They must agree to be alert to the temptation of developing a codependent relationship with members of their group.

Senior Pastor Support

The third key for growth in your recovery ministry is senior pastor support. I can't emphasize the importance of this key enough. In 1993, Pastor Rick took the entire church through a eight-week study of recovery based on the Beatitudes, and Celebrate Recovery took off!

Ezra 10:4 (TLB) says, "Take courage and tell us how to proceed in setting things straight, and we will fully cooperate." The people at Saddleback did cooperate, and the ministry not only grew but became a part of the church family. Your senior pastor's

---

[1]Because we encourage leaders to always share their hopes and victories with their Friday night groups, they understand that if they have had a tough week and feel that they are unable to lead their Friday night group with encouragement and hope, they can come to me before the meeting and I will find a replacement for them for that evening.

I tell them that I see their admission of a struggle as a strength not as a weakness. I will meet with them during the upcoming week to encourage them. Usually by the next Friday night they are back leading their group, sharing Christ's hope and power with a new enthusiasm and compassion.

support of your recovery program makes it acceptable for someone to be in recovery. It is not just "those" people, anymore—it's "us"![2]

In addition, your recovery ministry needs to participate in providing a service to the church other than its main purpose. If you want your recovery program to be respected and supported by the church as a whole, it needs to be and act as a regular ministry of the church, not as something separate. Celebrate Recovery participates in all churchwide events. For instance, we have a food booth at Western Day, a food booth and a game booth at the Harvest Party, and we sponsor the sock hop at the church's New Year's Eve Party.

Fellowship Events

The fourth key area for growth is fellowship events.

> Two are better than one, because they have a good return for their work: If one falls down, his friend can help him up. But pity the man who falls and has no one to help him up! . . . Though one may be overpowered, two can defend themselves. A cord of three strands is not quickly broken. *(Ecclesiastes 4:9–10, 12)*

It was not that many years ago that those in recovery were viewed by others as lacking the courage to seek help for their life's problems. Some of the early AA meetings were held in church basements, where members would enter by the back door so that no one would see them and identify them as alcoholics. Thank God, those back-door days in the basements are gone. Your recovery program needs to be out in the open, a regular place where people in recovery can join together, fellowship with one another, and get God's answer on how to overcome their struggles by His power.

At Celebrate Recovery we have two main fellowship events, the Bar-B-Que and Solid Rock Cafe (see Appendix C). The Bar-B-Que starts at 6:00 P.M. every Friday night throughout the summer. Our menu includes Recovery Dogs, 12-Step Chicken, Serenity Sausages, and Denial Burgers. We have great prices and great fellowship! Solid Rock Cafe follows our small group time. It is a great place to "unofficially" continue the meeting.

At Celebrate Recovery, the main focus of every fellowship event is to help members develop healthy relationships that will grow into a support team of sponsors and accountability partners. Both the Bar-B-Que and Solid Rock Cafe are designed to encourage individuals to meet either before or after our Friday night meetings. They provide a forum for the building of accountability teams and sponsorship relationships. (We don't assign sponsors; it is each person's responsibility to find and establish that important and personal relationship.)

Curriculum

The fifth key for a successful recovery program is finding the right curriculum. The number-one question I get asked about starting a recovery ministry is "What is the best curriculum?"

---

[2]Dysfunctional families don't talk, don't trust, and don't feel. Safe families do talk, do trust, and do feel! The church is a family as well. It can be a dysfunctional family, in which you are not allowed to feel, to talk openly, or to trust others; or it can be a safe place, a healing place, in which members can express their feelings, talk openly, and trust that others will not judge them. What we don't talk out creatively, we will act out destructively. Your church needs to be a safe place!

There is a wide variety of resources from which to choose, but I believe the foundation for an effective recovery ministry curriculum should be the same: the Bible. God's Word needs to be at the center of your recovery program. And it can't be if it is not the center of your curriculum. (At Celebrate Recovery we use and supply the *Life Recovery Bible*.)

Romans 15:4 tells us, "For everything that was written in the past was written to teach us, so that through endurance and the encouragement of the Scriptures we might have hope." The Big Book of Alcoholics Anonymous contains twelve great promises, but God's Big Book—God's love letter to us—has over seven thousand miraculous promises!

Second, make sure your curriculum can be applied to all groups—all areas of recovery. If it is biblically based, it will! At Celebrate Recovery, we want to try to break the family's cycle of dysfunction at the youngest level—the kids. That's why we have "Celebrate Kids," a program for children ages five through eleven whose parents are in recovery. We also offer a program for parents that runs twice a year for six weeks called "Recovering with Your Kids."

A third thing to look for in choosing a curriculum is its usability: Is the curriculum easy to use? Remember, it's impossible to eat an elephant in one bite, but if you cut it up in small pieces it becomes much easier (though not necessarily any tastier!).

Fourth, the material needs to create movement through the steps. Some books do a great job of teaching *about* the twelve steps and specific areas of recovery; however, they do not encourage movement *through* the steps. I have seen many individuals get to the fourth step and get bogged down, dwelling in the mud of their past. Even worse, they judge the program as too hard and stop the recovery process altogether!

The Celebrate Recovery curriculum fills all four of these curriculum requirements: It is built on God's Word; it can be used in all areas of recovery; it is packaged in four easy-to use, bite-size participant's guides and completing each of the books gives a sense of progress and assurance of movement through the steps and principles.

New Groups

The sixth key for growing your recovery ministry is building new groups. Built around individual needs and recovery issues, new groups act like blood transfusions in your recovery ministry. People gain a sense of excitement and enthusiasm when a new group starts. Second Corinthians 9:12 says, "This service that you perform is not only supplying the needs of God's people but is also overflowing in many expressions of thanks to God."

I would, however, like to offer a word of caution: *Start your recovery ministry off slowly*. I guarantee you that you will have masses of people coming to you saying, "Why don't you have a group for this addiction or this compulsion or behavior?" or "Don't you consider _____ as important as your chemically dependent group?" And being the compassionate person that you are, your first instinct will be to say, "We'll start it next week!" and then you go off and try to find someone to lead it.

That's the wrong way to start your recovery program. We started Celebrate with just four groups—Chemically Dependent Men, Chemically Dependent Women, Codependent Men, and Codependent Women. From there, I have used the following system for starting new groups.

When someone comes to me and asks why we don't have a group for "xyz" recovery, I usually respond, "Do you have any experience/recovery in that specific area?" (This experience could be Christ-centered or secular.) And then, "Do you know of anybody that has recovery in that area?" If the response to both of those questions is no, then I ask for the person's name and phone number and keep the information on file so that we can notify the person if and when that group starts.

Also, we do not start a new group until we have a trained leader and coleader, trained by the leader, in place. Once we have the leaders, we run announcements for the new group in the church bulletin for two weeks. Next, we have the leader and coleader give their testimonies in our Celebrate Recovery large group time. After completing that process, the new group begins meeting.

I can't tell you the number of women who asked me if we had a group for sexual and physical abuse. I had to say, "Not yet." It was *two years* before God sent us the right leadership team. I would rather disappoint someone by not having a group when they want it than cause someone great harm by having a group without trained and qualified leaders.

Outreach

The last of the seven keys for keeping your recovery ministry healthy and growing is outreach.

Matthew 5:14–16 tells us that we are to be "the light of the world. A city on a hill cannot be hidden. Neither do people light a lamp and put it under a bowl. Instead they put it on its stand, and it gives light to everyone in the house. In the same way, let your light shine before men, that they may see your good deeds and praise your Father in heaven."

It's great to have Celebrate Recovery for those who attend Saddleback Church. So many of our new people come into the church full of the world and all its baggage. Celebrate Recovery provides a safe place for them to begin their journey of stepping out of their denial and into God's grace, as well as helping them to start dealing with their life's hurts, hang-ups, and habits.

While just "being" here is great, it falls short of putting our lamps on a stand and letting our light shine before men. So what are some areas of outreach for your recovery ministry to consider?

One way we have been successful is by starting meetings at local recovery houses. Currently we are working with two Christ-centered houses. They hold their own Celebrate Recovery meetings using our curriculum and also take vans to Celebrate Recovery meetings on Friday nights at Saddleback.

Another outreach opportunity is to help other churches start recovery ministries. There are several ways we do this.

First, we go to a local church with our Celebrate Recovery band and leadership team, and we spend the day giving testimonies and teaching on the third principle: "Consciously choose to commit all my life and will to Christ's care and control." This attracts church members who are already attending secular recovery programs or Christ-centered recovery programs at other churches.

Pastors have often said to me, "We don't have those kinds of problems in my church." When I hear this, I say a short, silent prayer and then smile and respond, "Keep coming back." The truth of the matter is that every church has people in it who have had years of experience with twelve-step recovery programs and who could help you lead this kind of ministry. They are just waiting until they know it's safe to come forward and serve.

The second way we have helped local churches is by having their leadership attend Celebrate Recovery meetings at Saddleback Church for several weeks. We encourage them to take what they like and leave what they don't.

The third opportunity of outreach is to send out short-term mission teams. In 1994 I had the privilege of leading a Celebrate Recovery team to the Ukraine and Russia. We put on a Celebrate Recovery seminar at New Life Church in Kiev that was attended by forty village churches. The Celebrate Recovery material was translated into Russian and is being used today.

Once you let the light of the Lord shine, it keeps shining. Let me share with you an excerpt from a recent letter that I received as a result of our work in Russia:

> My family and I have been missionaries in Portugal for the past eight years. We have been working in church planting ... where there is very little evangelical witness. We have been involved in the area of recovery (especially of drug and alcohol abuse) in our cross-cultural setting. I was very impressed with the work done by Saddleback in October 1994 for the New Life Church Pastor's Conference in Kiev, Ukraine. We received a copy of the printed material used in the conference.
>
> At this time we are working with a Portuguese doctor who has two twelve-step clinics here in Portugal. He and his family will be visiting the Southern California area with us this summer. Could you please set aside a little time in August to meet with us and to explain the Recovery program at Saddleback? ... We would deeply appreciate it.

The fourth suggestion is to inform local Christian counselors about your program. At Saddleback we have a list of church-approved Christian counselors and therapists who have been interviewed by five staff pastors to insure that their counseling is built on God's Word and not on the world. We work very closely with these counselors and they refer many of their clients from other churches and those with no church affiliation to Celebrate Recovery.

Yet another suggestion is to invite guest speakers. Dr. John Townsend, Dr. Henry Cloud, and Steven Arterburn are regular guest speakers at Celebrate Recovery, and when they come our attendance increases by twenty percent. I try to have a guest speaker once per quarter. Not only does this attract new people, it's a refreshing change for the members of Celebrate.

The last outreach opportunity is to encourage your members to attend secular recovery meetings and share the one and only true Higher Power, Jesus Christ! We can't wait for the unsaved to come to us. We need to get out and reach them where they are! Remember, "Let your light shine before men, that they may see your good deeds and praise your Father in heaven" (Matthew 5:16).

III. Meeting Formats and Materials

This section will provide you with the "nuts and bolts" of starting and running an ongoing recovery ministry.

One-year Large Group Teaching Schedule and Curriculum Plan

First, we will look at the one-year large group teaching schedule and curriculum plan. This plan is designed to cover the twenty-five lessons in the four participant's guides—all of the eight principles and twelve steps—over a one-year period. A lesson is taught one week and then supported by a testimony or other special service the following week.[3] Please remember, however, that everyone works through the principles and steps at their own speed—twelve to eighteen months is not uncommon.

Participant's Guide 1: Stepping Out of Denial Into God's Grace

Week	Principle	Large Group Teaching
1		Introduction of Program
2	1	Lesson 1: Denial
3	1	Testimony
4	1	Lesson 2: Powerless
5	1	Testimony
6	2	Lesson 3: Hope
7	2	Testimony
8	2	Special music or outside speaker
9	2	Lesson 4: Sanity
10	2	Testimony
11	3	Lesson 5: Turn
12	3	Testimony
13	3	Lesson 6: Action
14	3	Communion

Participant's Guide 2: Taking an Honest and Spiritual Inventory

Week	Principle	Large Group Teaching
15	4	Lesson 7: Moral
16	4	Testimony
17	4	Lesson 8: Sponsor
18	4	Testimony
19	4	Lesson 9: Inventory
20	4	Testimony
21	4	Special Music or Outside Speaker
22	4	Lesson 10: Spiritual Inventory (Part 1)
23	4	Testimony
24	4	Lesson 11: Spiritual Inventory (Part 2)

[3]Several testimonies are included in this leader's guide. Use them as examples to guide you as you choose members from your own group to share their stories, read them aloud in your group, or use them for your own enrichment and encouragement.

Participant's Guide 3: Getting Right with God, Yourself, and Others

Week	Principle	Large Group Teaching
25	4	Lesson 12: Confess
26	4	Testimony
27	4	Lesson 13: Admit
28	4	Testimony
29	5	Lesson 14: Ready
30	5	Testimony
31	5	Lesson 15: Victory
32	5	Testimony
33	6	Lesson 16: Amends
34	6	Testimony
35	6	Lesson 17: Forgiveness
36	6	Testimony
37	6	Lesson 18: Grace
38	6	Testimony
39	6	Special Music and Communion

Participant's Guide 4: Growing in Christ While Helping Others

Week	Principle	Large Group Teaching
40	7	Lesson 19: Crossroads
41	7	Testimony
42	7	Lesson 20: Daily Inventory
43	7	Testimony
44	7	Lesson 21: Relapse
45	7	Testimony
46	7	Lesson 22: Gratitude
47	7	Testimony
48	8	Lesson 23: Give
49	8	Testimony
50	8	Lesson 24: Yes
51	8	Testimony
52		Lesson 25: The Seven Reasons We Get Stuck

Since individuals will join the program at different times throughout the year, you need to caution them against trying to catch up with the teaching. If a newcomer enters the program during week 35, for example, when you are teaching on Principle 6, he or she should still begin in Participant's Guide 1, *Stepping Out of Denial Into God's Grace*, working on Principle 1. Newcomers need to understand that this is an ongoing program and that they need to work through the principles at their own speed. What they are learning in the large group teaching time will be extremely valuable to them when they get to each particular principle.

Meeting Format: Large Group Worship and Teaching Time

The large group worship and teaching time at Celebrate Recovery is designed to enable those attending to set aside the busyness and the stresses of the outside world by participating in a twenty-minute time of prayer, praise, and worship. This time begins to unfold the "safe" environment that is essential to any recovery program and allows all those present to get in touch with the one and only Higher Power, Jesus Christ.

Praise the LORD. Praise God in his sanctuary; praise him in his mighty heavens. Praise him for his acts of power; praise him for his surpassing greatness. Praise him with the sounding of the trumpet, praise him with the harp and lyre, praise him with tambourine and dancing, praise him with the strings and flute, praise him with the clash of cymbals, praise him with resounding cymbals. Let everything that has breath praise the LORD. Praise the LORD. *(Psalm 150:1–6)*

Following is the agenda for Celebrate Recovery's large group worship and teaching time:

6:30 P.M.	Doors open—greeters in place
7:00 P.M.	Opening song
	Welcome and opening prayer
7:05 P.M.	Song #2
	Song #3
	Song #4
7:20 P.M.	Reading of the eight principles and their corresponding Beatitudes or the twelve steps and their biblical comparisons
7:25 P.M.	Announcements
7:30 P.M.	Special music
7:35 P.M.	Teaching or testimony
7:50 P.M.	Serenity prayer
	Closing song
7:55 P.M.	Dismissal to small groups

Greeters

Greeters are extremely important in both making a positive first impression on all newcomers and in encouraging regular attendees. In addition to greeting, the greeters also hand out the Celebrate Recovery bulletin for the evening.

The Celebrate Recovery Bulletin

The Celebrate Recovery bulletin contains the following information:

Song sheet
Small group meeting room assignments
Solid Rock Cafe/Bar-B-Que information sheets
Small group meeting guidelines
Twelve steps and their biblical comparisons
List of weekly small group meetings
Announcements of upcoming special events

A sample bulletin (jacket and inside pages) as well as examples of some of the above elements can be found in Appendix D.

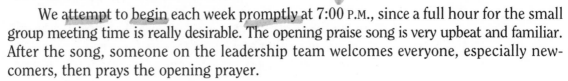

Opening Song, Welcome, and Prayer

We attempt to begin each week promptly at 7:00 P.M., since a full hour for the small group meeting time is really desirable. The opening praise song is very upbeat and familiar. After the song, someone on the leadership team welcomes everyone, especially newcomers, then prays the opening prayer.

Set of Three Songs

The music continues with songs chosen to go along with the particular principle the group will be working on that evening.

Some examples would be:

Principle 1: "The Power of Your Love"
Principle 2: "I Have a Hope"
Principle 3: "Jesus Is the Answer"
Principle 4: "Fear Not"; "White as Snow"
Principle 5: "Cry of My Heart"; "Change My Heart, Oh God"
Principle 6: "God Can Make It Right"; "Mourning Into Dancing"
Principle 7: "Search Me, Oh God"; "More of You in My Life"
Principle 8: "The Road to Recovery"

This praise and worship time is extremely important!

Reading of the Eight Principles and their corresponding Beatitude or the Twelve Steps and Their Biblical Comparisons

The eight principles or the twelve steps and their biblical comparisons are read at every meeting. The purpose is twofold: (1) to reinforce the biblical foundation for the program, and (2) to allow increased participation for Celebrate Recovery attendees.

One person is asked to read the principle/step and another reads the Bible verse for that step until all eight principles/twelve steps are completed.

Example:

First reader: "Principle 1: Realize I'm not God. I admit that I am powerless to control my tendency to do the wrong thing and that my life is unmanageable."

Second reader: "Happy are those who know they are spiritually poor" (Matthew 5:3 GNB).

The opportunity to read is used to reward regular attendees and encourage prospective new coleaders.

Announcements

The purpose of the announcements is to help the newcomers feel welcome and inform them about the meeting rooms and where to get their questions answered. While an important part of the program, announcements can be rather "dry" (to be kind), so we attempt to make them light and fun. The remainder of the time is used to announce upcoming events and introduce the "special music" for the evening.

Special Music

Special music supports the teaching or the testimony for the evening. It is usually a solo performed by one of the Celebrate Recovery Singers. In the past we used to bring in outside singers from other groups in the church, but we have found that the group really enjoys supporting "one of their own."

Also, during the special music selection a collection, or "love offering," can be taken. The money collected could be used to support recovery mission trips, to pay for special speakers, and to offset the cost of outreach programs to other area churches.

Teaching or Testimony

As mentioned previously, we teach the twenty-five lessons from the participant's guides over the calendar year. Typically, we follow a teaching week with a testimony week, which supports the teaching of the previous lesson.

Serenity Prayer, Closing Song, and Dismissal to Small Groups

The large group meeting ends with one of the leaders leading the group in the reading of the complete version of Reinhold Neibuhr's Serenity Prayer. The prayer is printed on the inside cover of the bulletin jacket (see Appendix D). Then we have the closing song and everyone is encouraged to quickly go to their small group meetings located throughout the church campus. Meeting locations are also found in the bulletin.

Celebrate Recovery's Small Group Formats

Format One: For small groups following the large group worship and teaching program

8:00 P.M.	Opening prayer and welcome
	Introductions
	Reading of Celebrate Recovery's small group meeting guidelines
8:05 P.M.	Leader's focus on the principle
8:10 P.M.	Group discussion and open sharing
8:50 P.M.	Wrap-up, prayer requests, closing prayer
9:00 P.M.	Invitation to the Solid Rock Cafe

Opening Prayer, Welcome, and Introductions

This time allows the small group to again focus their attention to the Lord and to feel the bond of their small group. It is also another opportunity to softly welcome newcomers.

Reading of Celebrate Recovery's Small Group Meeting Guidelines

These small group guidelines (see Appendix E) are read at every small group meeting. They are five simple rules that will keep the group *safe!* If your recovery meetings are not safe, they will fail! It is the responsibility of the group leader and coleader to insure that these guidelines are followed. To reinforce their importance, the guidelines are also read every four to six weeks during the large group time.

Leader's Focus on the Principle

The leader spends just a few minutes on going over the key points from the evening's lesson and then asks the group to start their sharing about one or two of the questions from the lesson's exercise. For example, the leader would ask the group the question from Principle 1 of the *Stepping Out of Denial Into God's Grace* Participant's Guide: "What areas of your life do you have power (control) over?"

Group Discussion and Open Sharing

The group should begin with focused disc[...] naturally transfer into open sharing.

Wrap-up, Prayer Requests, Closing Prayer

*Wrapping up the session is the leader's r[...] that the group has enough time for closure—[...] an abrupt halt or go on and on and on. Befor[...] time for group members to give specific pray[...] prayer. If there were any major issues raised i[...] get the individual's name for follow-up.

Invitation to the Solid Rock Cafe

The meeting can now continue "unofficially" at the Solid Rock Cafe, a place designed specifically for fellowship. At the cafe, individuals have an opportunity to continue to share with those with whom they feel safe. It is a time for group members to develop accountability partners and sponsorship relationships.

Format Two: for small groups meeting throughout the week

7:00 P.M.	Opening prayer and welcome
	Introductions
	Serenity Prayer
	Reading of the eight principles and/or the twelve steps and their biblical comparisons
	Reading of Celebrate Recovery's small group meeting guidelines
	Leader's focus on the principle or topic
7:15 P.M.	Group discussion and open sharing
8:50 P.M.	Wrap-up, prayer requests, closing prayer
9:00 P.M.	Closing[4]

The Information Table and Materials

The information table is a key part of helping the newcomer feel welcome. The table's location is very important. After the greeter, it should be the next experience for newcomers. They do not have to go to it upon their arrival, but it is important that they know its location.

The table should be staffed by at least one man and one woman. We do this to be sensitive to those in attendance. A woman with abuse issues, for example, would find it difficult to seek information from a man. Also, it is important to have an information table leader who is responsible for staffing the table, maintaining fresh handouts, and for administrating curriculum and Bible sales.

[4]There are only two points at which this format and Format One differ. In Format Two, the small groups recite the Serenity Prayer and read the eight principles and/or the twelve steps and their biblical comparisons. This is unnecessary in Format One because these two elements are covered in the large group meeting directly prior to the small group session.

...andouts should be colorful and have some uniformity. We stock the following
...s at our Celebrate Recovery information table:

Welcome Newcomers
Road to Recovery
8 Recovery Principles Based on the Beatitudes
12 Steps for Sexual and Physical Abuse
12 Steps for the Addicted and Compulsive Person*[5]
Things We Are ... Things We Are Not*
Codependency and Christian Living*
Enabling*
Compliance Patterns*
What is Codependency?*
Renewal from Sexual Addiction
Eating Disorder Group
Welcome Home
C.O.S.A. Spouse's Group
Special Announcements of Upcoming Events

(For examples of these handouts, see Appendix F.)

How This Leader's Guide Is Organized

As stated earlier, this leader's guide is designed to cover the twenty-five sessions
in the four participant's guides—all of the eight principles. As you prepare, please feel
free to use any or all of the lesson provided. I have written the lesson so that you can
either read it in its entirety or "cut and paste" with your own illustrations and just follow
the basic format. Use the guide to best meet the needs of your group. May God bless
you and your ministry as you lead others down the road to recovery.

[5]Handouts designated by an asterisk may not be copied. They have been given to me throughout
the years, and I do not know their authors. I would love to give them credit for their great contributions.
They have really helped our ministry.

Principle 1

Realize I'm not God. I admit that I am powerless to control my tendency to do the wrong thing and that my life is unmanageable.

"Happy are those who know they are spiritually poor."

Denial

Principle 1: Realize I'm not God. I admit that I am powerless to control my tendency to do the wrong thing and that my life is unmanageable.

Happy are those who know they are spiritually poor.

Step 1: We admitted we were powerless over our addictions and compulsive behaviors, that our lives had become unmanageable.

I know that nothing good lives in me, that is, in my sinful nature. For I have the desire to do what is good, but I cannot carry it out.

Romans 7:18

Introduction

Tonight we begin a journey together, a journey down the road of recovery. This journey begins with Principle 1, where we admit that we are powerless to control our tendency to do the wrong thing and that our lives have become unmanageable, out of control. But before we begin this exciting journey together, we need to ask ourselves two questions:

> • Am I going to let my past failures prevent me from taking this journey?

> • Am I afraid to change? Or, what are my fears of the future?

Failures from the Past

Let's look at Hebrews 12:1 (TLB):

Since we have such a huge crowd of men of faith watching us from the grandstands, let us strip off anything that slows us down or holds us back, and especially those sins that wrap themselves so tightly around our feet and trip us up; and let us run with patience the particular race that God has set before us.

There are two things I would like to point out in this verse. First, God has a particular race, a unique plan, for each of us. A plan for good, not a life full of dependencies, addictions, and obsessions.

The second thing is that *we need to be willing* to get rid of all the unnecessary baggage, the past failures, in our lives that keep us stuck. Again, it says, "Let us strip off anything that slows us down or holds us back, and especially those sins that wrap themselves so tightly around our feet and trip us up."

For many of us, our past hurts, hang-ups, and habits hold us back, trip us up! Many of us are stuck in bitterness over what someone has done to us. We continue to hold on to the hurt and we refuse to forgive the ones who had hurt us.

You may have been hurt deeply. Perhaps you were abused as a child, or maybe you were or are in a marriage where your spouse committed adultery.

I want you to know that I hurt for you. I'm truly sorry for you, sorry that you had to go through that hurt. But holding on to that hurt and not being willing to forgive the person who hurt you in the past is allowing them to continue to hurt you today, in the present.

Working this Christ-centered recovery program will, with God's power, allow you to find the courage and strength to forgive them. Now don't get all stressed out. You don't have to forgive them tonight! But as you travel down your road to recovery, God will help you find the willingness to forgive them and be free of their hold on your life.

Some of you are bound by guilt. You keep beating yourself up over some past failure. You're trapped, stuck in your guilt. You think that no one anywhere is as bad as you are, that no one could love the *real* you, and that no one could ever forgive you for the terrible things that you have done.

You're wrong. God can. That's why Jesus went to the cross, for our sins. He knows everything you've ever done and everything you've ever experienced.

And there are many here tonight that have faced similar failures and hurts in their life and have accepted Christ's forgiveness. They are here to encourage and support you.

The apostle Paul had a lot to regret about his past. He even participated in Stephen's murder. Yet in Philippians 3:13 (TLB) he tells us, "No, dear brothers, I am still not all I should be but I am bringing all my energies to bear on this one thing: Forgetting the past and looking forward to what lies ahead."

Here's the bottom line if you want to be free from your past hurts, hang-ups, and habits: You need to deal with your past bitterness and guilt once and for all. You need to do as Isaiah 43:18 tells us, "Forget the former things; do not dwell on the past." That doesn't mean *ignore* the past. You need to *learn* from your past, offer forgiveness, make amends, and then release it. Only then can you be free from your guilt, grudges, and grief!

Let's face it, we have all stumbled over a hurt, hang-up, or habit. But the race isn't over yet. God isn't interested in how we started, but how we finish the race.

Fears for the Future

You may worry about your future and are afraid to change. We all worry about things that we do not have any control over and do not have the power to change. And we all know worrying is a lack of trust in God.

The truth is, we can say without any doubt or fear, "The Lord is my Helper and I am not afraid of anything that mere man can do to me" (Hebrews 13:6 TLB).

You may have been in your hurt, habit, or hang-up for so long that it has become your identity. You may be thinking, "What will happen if I really give recovery a chance? Will I change? If I give up my old hurts, hang-ups, and habits, what will I become? Who will I be?"

You may have been abusing alcohol, prescription drugs, or food. You're afraid of what you will do without your substance of choice.

You may have been enabling someone in a dysfunctional relationship for years. Perhaps you wonder, "What if I change and my alcoholic husband gets mad at me?"

God doesn't want you to stay frozen in an unhealthy relationship or a bad habit. He wants you to do your part in becoming healthy.

Even if our past was extremely painful, however, we may still resist change and the freedom that can be found in really working this program. Because of our fear of the unknown or because of our despair, we just close our minds because we think that we don't deserve any better.

As you work the steps remember 1 John 4:18 (NCV): "Where God's love is, there is no fear, because God's perfect love drives out fear."

You are not here by mistake tonight. This room is full of changed lives. It is my prayer for each of you that you will not let your past failures or your fear of your future stop you from giving Celebrate Recovery a real try.

Are you wearing a mask of denial tonight? Before you can make any progress in your recovery, you need to face your denial. As soon as you remove your mask, your recovery begins—or begins again! It doesn't matter if you're new in recovery or have been in recovery, working the steps for years. Denial can rear its ugly head and return at any time! You may trade addictions or get into a new relationship that's unhealthy for you in a different way than the previous one. So this lesson is for all of us.

We have a saying around here: "Denial isn't just a river in Egypt." But what is it?

What Is Denial?

Denial has been defined as "a false system of beliefs that are not based on reality" and "a self-protecting behavior that keeps us from honestly facing the truth."

As kids we all learned various coping skills. They came in handy when we didn't get the attention we wanted from our parents and others or to block our pain and our fears.

For a time these coping systems worked. But as the years progressed they confused and clouded our view of the truth of our lives.

As we grew, our perception of ourselves and our expectations of all those around us also grew. But because we retained our childish methods of coping, our perceptions of reality became increasingly more unrealistic and distorted.

Our coping skills grew into denial, and most of our relationships ended up broken or less fulfilling than they could have been.

Did you ever deny that your parents had problems? Did you ever deny that you had problems? The truth is, we can all answer yes to these questions to some extent. But, for some of us, that denial turned to shame and guilt.

Denial is the "Pink Elephant" sitting in the middle of the living room. No one in the family talks about it or acknowledges it in any way. Do any of the following comments sound familiar to you?

- "Can't we stop talking about it? Talking only makes it worse."

- "Billy, if we *don't* talk about it, it will go away."

- "Honey, let's pretend that it didn't really happen."

- "If I tell her that it hurts me when she says that, I'm afraid she will leave me."

- "He really doesn't drink that much."

- "It really doesn't hurt when he does that; I'm fine!"

- "Paul drinks more than I do."

- "Joan has been married three times; I've only been married twice."

- "I eat because you make me so mad!"

- "If you didn't nag me all the time, I wouldn't . . ."

- "Look honey, I have a tough job; I work hard. I need a few drinks to relax. It doesn't mean that I have a problem."

Folks, that's DENIAL.

As I said earlier, before we can take the first step of our recovery, we must first face and admit our denial. God says in Jeremiah 6:14 (TLB), "You can't heal a wound by saying it's not there!"

Effects of Denial

Okay, let's look at tonight's acrostic:

DENIAL

Disables our feelings
Energy lost
Negates growth
Isolates us from God
Alienates us from our relationships
Lengthens the pain

The *D* in denial stands for DISABLES our feelings. Hiding our feelings, living in denial, freezes our emotions and binds us. Understanding and feeling our feelings is where we find freedom.

Second Peter 2:19 (GNB) tells us: "They promise them freedom, while they themselves are slaves of destructive habits—for a man is a slave of anything that has conquered him."

For me, the basic test of freedom is not what I'm free to do, it's what I'm free not to do! I'm free not to take that drink.

We find freedom to feel our true feelings when we find Christ and step out of denial.

The next letter in denial is *E*, which stands for ENERGY lost.

A major side-effect of denial is anxiety. Anxiety causes us to waste precious energy dealing with past hurts and failures and the fear of the future. As you go though this program you will learn that it is only in the present that positive change can occur. Worrying about the past and dreading the future makes us unable to live and enjoy God's plans for us in the present.

We let our fears and our worries paralyze us, but the only lasting way we can be free from them is by giving them to God. Psalm 146:7 (TLB) says, "He frees the prisoners, . . . he lifts the burdens from those bent down beneath their loads."

If you will transfer the energy required to maintain your denial into learning God's truth, a healthy love for others and yourself will occur. As you depend more and more on your Higher Power, Jesus Christ, you will see the light of truth and reality.

Let's move on to the *N* in denial.

Denial NEGATES growth.

We are as sick as our secrets and, again, we cannot grow in recovery until we are ready to step out of our denial into the truth. God is waiting to take your hand and bring you out. The Bible says, "They cried to the Lord in their troubles, and he rescued them! He led them from the darkness and shadow of death and snapped their chains" (Psalm 107:13–14 TLB).

As you travel the road of your recovery you will come to understand that God never wastes a hurt; God will never waste your darkness. But He can't use it unless you step out of your denial into the light of His truth.

Denial also ISOLATES us from God.

Adam and Eve are a great example of how secrets and denial separate us from true fellowship with God. After they sinned, their secret separated them from God. Genesis 3:7 tells us that Adam and Eve hid from God because they felt naked and ashamed.

Of course, good old Adam tried to rationalize. He said to God, "The woman you put here with me—she gave me some fruit from the tree" (Genesis 3:12). First he tried to blame God, saying, "The woman you put here with me . . ." Then he tried to blame it on Eve: "*She* gave me some fruit."

Remember, God's light shines on the truth. Our denial keeps us in the dark. "God is light, in him there is no darkness at all. If we claim to have fellowship with him and yet walk in the darkness, we lie and do not live by the truth. But if we walk in the light, as he is in the light, we have fellowship with one another, and the blood of Jesus, his Son, purifies us from all sin" (1 John 1:5–7).

Our denial not only isolates us from God, it ALIENATES us from our relationships.

Denial tells us we are getting away with it. We think no one knows, but they do. But while denial may shield us from the hurt, it also keeps us from helping ourselves or the people we love the most. We don't dare reveal our true selves to others for fear of what they will think or say if they knew the real us. We must protect ourselves—our secrets—at any cost. So we isolate ourselves and thereby minimize the risk of exposure and possible rejection from others. But at what price? The eventual loss of all our important relationships.

What's the answer? Listen to Ephesians 4:25 (LB). "Stop lying to each other; tell the truth, for we are parts of each other and when we lie to each other we are hurting ourselves."

Remember it is always better to tell the ugly truth rather than a beautiful lie.

Finally, denial LENGTHENS the pain.

We have the false belief that denial protects us from our pain. In reality, denial allows our pain to fester and grow and to turn into shame and guilt. Denial extends your hurt. It multiplies your problems.

Truth, like surgery, may hurt for a while, but it cures. God promises us in Jeremiah 30:17 (TLB), "I will give you back your health again and heal your wounds."

Wrap-up

Tonight I encourage you to *step out* of your denial! Walking out of your denial is not easy. Taking off that mask is hard. Everything about you shouts, "Don't do it! It's not safe!" But it is safe. It's safe at Celebrate Recovery. Here you have people who care about you and who love you for who you are—people who will stand beside you as truth becomes a way of life.

Jesus tells us, "Know the truth, and the truth will set you free" (John 8:32). Step out of your denial so you can step into Jesus' unconditional love and grace and begin your healing journey of recovery.

Powerless

Principle 1: Realize I'm not God. I admit that I am powerless to control my tendency to do the wrong thing and that my life is unmanageable.

Happy are those who know they are spiritually poor.

Step 1: We admitted we were powerless over our addictions and compulsive behaviors, that our lives had become unmanageable.

I know that nothing good lives in me, that is, in my sinful nature. For I have the desire to do what is good, but I cannot carry it out.
Romans 7:18

Introduction

In Principle 1, we realize we're not God. We admit we are powerless to control our tendency to do the wrong thing and that our lives have become unmanageable. As soon as we take this step and admit that we are powerless, we start to change. We see that our old ways of trying to control our hurts, hang-ups, and habits didn't work. They were buried by our denial and held on to with our false power.

Tonight we are going to focus on four actions: <u>two things we have to *stop* doing</u> and <u>two things we need to *start* doing</u> in our recoveries. We need to take these four actions to complete Principle 1.

Four Actions

In Lesson 1 we talked about the first action we need to take.

1. Stop denying the pain.

We said that our denial had at least six negative effects: It disables our feelings, wastes our energy, negates our growth, isolates us from God, alienates us from our relationships, and lengthens our pain.

You are ready to accept Principle 1 when your pain is greater than your fear. In Psalm 6:2–3 (TLB) David talks about a time when he came to the end of his emotional and physical resources: "Pity me, O LORD, for I am weak. Heal me, for my body is sick, and I am upset and disturbed. My mind is filled with apprehension and with gloom." When David's pain finally surpassed his fear, he was able to face his denial and feel the reality of his pain. In the same way, if you want to be rid of your pain, you must face it and go through it.

The second action we need to take is to

2. Stop playing God.

You are either going to serve God or self. You can't do both! Matthew 6:24 (GNB) says, "No one can be a slave to two masters; he will hate one and love the other; he will be loyal to one and despise the other."

Another term for serving "ourselves" is serving the "flesh." Flesh is the Bible's word for our unperfected human nature, our sin nature.

I love this illustration: If you leave the *h* off the end of flesh and reverse the remaining letters, you spell the word *self*. Flesh is the self-life. It is what we are when we are left to our own devices.

The Big Book of AA describes the alcoholic as a person whose self-will has run riot! When "self" is out of control, all attempts at control—of self or others—fail. In fact, our attempt to control ourselves and others is what got us into trouble in the first place. God needs to be the one in control.

There are two jobs: God's and mine! We have been trying to do God's job, and we can't!

On the flip side, He *won't* do our job. We need to do the footwork! We need to admit that we are not God and that our lives are unmanageable without Him. Then, when we have finally emptied ourselves, God will have room to come in and begin His healing work.

Let's go on now to the third action we need to take:

3. Start admitting our powerlessness.

The lust of power is not rooted in our strengths but our weaknesses. We need to realize our human weaknesses and quit trying to do it by ourselves. We need to admit that we are powerless and turn our lives over to God. Jesus knew how difficult this is. He said, "With man this is impossible, but with God all things are possible" (Matthew 19:26).

When we keep doing things that we don't want to do and when we fail to do the things we've decided we need to do, we begin to see that we do not, in fact, have the power to change that we thought we had. Life is coming into focus more clearly than ever before.

The last action we need to take is to

4. Start admitting that our lives have become unmanageable.

The only reason we consider that there's something wrong, or that we need to talk to somebody, or that we need to take this step is because we finally are able to admit that some area—or all areas—of our lives have become unmanageable!

It is with this admission that you finally realize you are out of control and are powerless to do anything on your own. When I got to this part of my recovery I shared David's feelings that he expressed in Psalm 40:12 (TLB): "Problems far too big for me to solve are piled higher than my head. Meanwhile my sins, too many to count, have all caught up with me and I am ashamed to look up."

Does that sound familiar? Only when your pain is greater than your fear will you be ready to honestly take the first step, admitting that you are powerless and your life is unmanageable.

Tonight our acrostic will help us to focus in on the first half of Principle 1: powerless.

Powerless

Our acrostic tonight demonstrates what happens when we admit we are POWERLESS. We begin to give up the following "serenity robbers":

Pride

Only ifs

Worry

Escape

Resentment

Loneliness

Emptiness

Selfishness

Separation

The first letter in tonight's acrostic is *P*. We start to see that we no longer are trapped by our PRIDE: "Pride ends in a fall, while humility brings honor" (Proverbs 29:23 TLB).

Ignorance + power + pride = a deadly mixture

Our false pride undermines our faith and it cuts us off from God and others. When God's presence is welcome, there is no room for pride because He makes us aware of our true self.

Next we begin to lose the ONLY ifs. Have you ever had a case of the "only ifs"?

Only if they hadn't walked out ...

Only if I had stopped drinking....

Only if this ... Only if that....

How reluctantly the mind consents to reality. But when we admit that we are powerless, we start walking in the truth, rather than living in the fantasy land of rationalization.

Luke 12:2–3 (GNB) tells us: "Whatever is covered up will be uncovered, and every secret will be made known. So then, whatever you have said in the dark will be heard in broad daylight."

The next letter in powerless is the *W*, which stands for WORRYING. And don't tell me that worrying doesn't do any good; I know better. The things I worry about never happen!

All worrying is a form of not trusting God enough! Instead of worrying about things that we cannot possibly do, we need to focus on what God can do. Keep a copy of the Serenity Prayer in your pocket and your heart to remind you.

By working this program and completing the steps you can find that trust, that relationship, with the one and only Higher Power, Jesus Christ, so that the worrying begins to go away.

Matthew 6:34 (TLB) tells us, "Don't be anxious about tomorrow. God will take care of your tomorrow too. Live one day at a time."

The next thing that happens when we admit we are powerless is that we quit trying to ESCAPE.

Before we admitted we were powerless, we tried to escape and hide from our hurts, habits, and hang-ups by getting involved in unhealthy relationships, by abusing drugs such as alcohol, by eating or not eating, and so forth.

Trying to escape pain drains us of precious energy. When we take this first step, however, God opens *true* escape routes to show His power and grace. "For the light is capable of showing up everything for what it really is. It is possible for the light to turn the thing it shines upon into light also" (Ephesians 5:13–14 PHILLIPS).

The *R* in powerless stands for RESENTMENTS.

If they are suppressed and allowed to fester, resentments can act like emotional cancer.

Paul tells us in Ephesians 4:26–27: "In your anger do not sin ...: Do not let the sun go down while you are still angry, and do not give the devil a foothold."

As you continue to work the principles, you will come to understand that in letting go of your resentments, by offering your forgiveness to those that have hurt you, you are not just freeing the person who harmed you, you are freeing you!

But if we try to maintain our false power, we become isolated and alone. That's the *L* in powerless: LONELINESS.

When you admit that you are powerless and start to face reality, you will find that you do not have to be alone.

Do you know that loneliness is a choice? In recovery and in Christ, you never have to walk alone again.

Do you know that caring for the lonely can cure loneliness? Get involved! Get involved in the church or in your neighborhood or here at Celebrate Recovery! If you become a regular here, I guarantee that you won't be lonely.

"Continue to love each other with true brotherly love. Don't forget to be kind to strangers, for some who have done this have entertained angels without realizing it!" (Hebrews 13:1–2 TLB).

When you admit you are powerless you also give up the EMPTINESS.

When you finally admit that you are truly powerless by yourself, that empty feeling deep inside—that cold wind that blows through you—will go away.

Jesus said, "My purpose is to give life in all its fullness" (John 10:10 TLB). So let Him fill the emptiness inside. Tell Him how you feel. He cares!

Next you will notice that you are becoming less self-centered.

The first *S* stands for SELFISHNESS.

I have known people that have come into recovery thinking that the Lord's Prayer was "Our Father who art in heaven . . . Give me . . . give me . . . give me!" Luke 17:33 (TLB) tells us, "Whoever clings to his life shall lose it, and whoever loses his life shall save it." Simply said, selfishness is at the heart of most problems between people.

The last thing that we give up when we admit that we are powerless is SEPARATION.

Some people talk about "finding" God—as if He could ever be lost.

Separation from God can feel real, but it is never permanent. Remember, He seeks the lost. When we can't find God, we need to ask ourselves, "Who moved?" I'll give you a hint. It wasn't God!

"For I am convinced that nothing can ever separate us from his love. Death can't, and life can't. The angels won't, and all the powers of hell itself cannot keep God's love away. . . . Nothing will ever be able to separate us from the love of God demonstrated by our Lord Jesus Christ when he died for us" (Romans 8:38–39 TLB).

Wrap-up

The power to change only comes from God's grace.

Are you ready to truly begin your journey of recovery? Are you ready to stop denying the pain? Are you ready to stop playing God? Are you ready to start admitting your powerlessness? To start admitting that your life has become unmanageable? If you are, share it with your group tonight.

I encourage you to start working and living this program in earnest. If we admit we are powerless, we need a power greater than ourselves to restore us. That power is your Higher Power—Jesus Christ!

Let's close in prayer.

Dear God, Your Word tells me that I can't heal my hurts, hang-ups, and habits by just saying that they are not there. Help me! Parts of my life, or all of my life, are out of control. I now know that I cannot "fix" myself. It seems the harder that I try to do the right thing the more I struggle. Lord, I want to step out of my denial into the truth. I pray for You to show me the way. In Your Son's name, AMEN.

PRINCIPLE 1 TESTIMONY

Hi, my name is John. I'm a believer who struggles with alcoholism. My story is all about God taking me back when I finally gave up on doing it my way. You see, I had a great start in life. I was raised in a good Christian home. I was the child prodigy in my church, and many predicted I would take over for Billy Graham when he retired. Later in life I earned a master's degree from Fuller Seminary. In essence, I was trained for a life of ministry.

I threw all of that away, however, for what the Bible calls "the lusts of the flesh" and what I thought was a call to freedom. How did that happen? As you will see, I made the mistake of thinking I was strong enough to live life on my own terms.

My earliest memories are about God and Jesus. I remember asking my dad, "Why doesn't everybody believe in Jesus? It's so easy." (At the time I was praying that Nikita Khrushchev would become a Christian.) My dad answered, "When you get older, you'll understand. It gets harder to believe." My dad meant no harm, but the mind of a seven-year-old is a tender thing. I took his observation as a mandate: If I was going to grow up, I was going to have doubts. Shortly thereafter, I began to lose confidence in my relationship with God.

The struggle to rediscover a simple childlike faith would be the defining theme of my life for the next forty years. I discovered binge drinking in college during my senior year. But the need to try and earn God's acceptance persisted. If anybody could get God to give them a standing ovation, I was going to be that man. I married a good Christian girl from a good Christian home and entered Fuller Seminary. I had been a lazy undergrad student. Consequently I had two things to prove: first that I was indeed the spiritual giant my dad and others had always expected me to be, and second, that my intellectual prowess had no equal. I graduated from Fuller with a 3.8 GPA, a master's degree in divinity, and some major anxiety attacks. You see, all that head knowledge was worthless because I was performing a religion for God instead of having a relationship with God.

My self-doubts about God's salvation had spread to all areas of my life. I had even begun to doubt my very manhood, so I entered therapy. There I found that much of my low self-esteem could be explained away by an overactive "inner parent" who constantly demanded perfection. Good sound psychology as far as it goes, but it fell short of the saving conclusion the Big Book states that we all have to make: "... any life run on self-will can hardly be a success." Jesus put it another way in the real Big Book, the Bible: "Whoever wants to save his life will lose it, but whoever loses his life for me and for the gospel will save it" (Mark 8:35).

After starting a Ph.D. program in historical theology, I left Fuller and joined the business world. About a year later, a woman who was like a second mother to me died suddenly of a brain tumor. In spite of my pleading with God, Jan died that night, and I completed my walk away from God. Instead of turning to God in this time of loss, I used that dear woman's death as a convenient excuse to give up on God and satisfy all of my pent-up desires for wine, women, and song.

I was riding high in 1984. I had plenty of money, a home in Anaheim Hills, and I was surrounded by women who were openly available. I began to commit adultery after nine years of marriage. My excuse for being unfaithful was that my wife was not "exciting" enough. Excuses helped me to justify a divorce. Excuses and alcohol always gave me a way to deny the pain and deny what I had become: totally self-centered and egotistical. I found a gorgeous girlfriend who looked good on my arm, and I went into party mode for the balance of the 80s. Alcohol and cocaine were the order of the day. Believe it or not, that gorgeous girlfriend became my wife and remains my wife to this day in spite of all the hurt and heartache I have caused in her life. In 1993 our daughter was born. My little girl made me start to realize that I was not the center of the universe. I knew my family should be the center, but I continued to drink and act like an irresponsible adolescent.

Finally, in early 1994, my wife told me enough was enough. That was my wake-up call. I knew I had to get my life together or I was going to lose my wife and my little girl, both of whom I loved with all of my heart. I stopped going out to the bars but continued to drink at home. Drinking became a way to pass out every night and perpetuate the denial that had become my existence.

It took another two years, but in March of 1996, at the urging of my wife, we started attending Saddleback. Every Sunday, always nursing a hangover, I would be moved to tears by the music. God, through Pastor Rick, would touch my heart with some observation from the Bible that all my "enormous" Bible study skills had never uncovered before.

One Sunday, another John from our Celebrate Recovery group gave his testimony. Like me, he was a functional alcoholic. His story and the ministry of this church made me start to hope again that it was possible to have a relationship with a God of love rather than a God of judgment.

June 11, 1996 was my first day of sobriety. I came to our recovery meeting with a feeling that there was no place else to go. If I mentioned all of the men in this group who have helped me on the road to recovery, we would be here a lot longer than the time I have been allotted! However, I have to mention my brother Kenny. That first night, with a lot of love and not a lot of formal education, Ken helped me, Mr. Intellectual, complete four-word sentences as I tried to explain why I was there.

On Day 8 I wrote this in my journal: "I am still searching for a God that I know is there. Perhaps my God is too small, perhaps He is not there. I fervently hope that is not true; I have nowhere else to go." I knew beyond any doubt that alcohol was just a symptom. I was in a life-or-death search for the God who could make sense out of my life. On June 26, after a short meeting with Pastor John, one verse he shared with me finally cut through all of my denial. It was Psalm 46:10: "Be still, and know that I am God." It was as if God was saying to me, "Stop trying to maintain the facade, stop making excuses for your life, that is why I died for you. Be still, relax, and accept My gift of freedom."

I came home to my Abba, my Daddy in heaven. Like the prodigal son who finally realized that being a servant in his father's house was much better than living like a pig on his own, I finally admitted how much I needed God's help to manage my life. When I did, He welcomed me home with great joy, and the party (Luke 15:23) God threw for me and my family was overwhelming. In less than a month, my wife and I were baptized together by Pastor John, joined Saddleback Church, and dedicated our little girl to God.

I continue to be amazed at the peace I feel as I learn to let go of my own control and allow God to direct me. For the first time in forty years, I am praying an adult version of the prayer I prayed at the age of seven: "God, thank You, life is so simple when I turn everything over to You." The belief of a child, tempered by forty years of life, gives me a peace and serenity that I never imagined possible.

Thank you.

Principle 2

Earnestly believe that God exists, that I matter to Him, and that He has the power to help me recover.

"Happy are those who mourn, for they shall be comforted."

Hope

Principle 2: Earnestly believe that God exists, that I matter to Him, and that He has the power to help me recover.

Happy are those who mourn, for they shall be comforted.

Step 2: We came to believe that a power greater than ourselves could restore us to sanity.

For it is God who works in you to will and to act according to his good purpose.

Philippians 2:13

Introduction

In Principle 2 we earnestly believe that God exists, that we matter to Him, and that He has the power to help us recover. Hebrews 11:6 tells us, "Anyone who comes to [God] must believe that he exists and that he rewards those who earnestly seek him." Psalm 62:5 says, "Find rest, O my soul, in God alone; my hope comes from him."

In the first principle, we admitted we were *powerless*. It is through this admission of our powerlessness that we are able to *believe* and *receive* God's power to help us recover. We do need to be careful, though, not to just cover the bottomless pit of our hurts, hang-ups, and habits with layers of denial or just try some quick-fix. Instead, we need to keep those hurts exposed to the light so that through God's power they can truly heal.

It's in the second principle that we come to believe God exists, that we are important to Him, and that we are able to find the one true Higher Power, Jesus Christ! We come to understand that God wants to fill our lives with His love, His joy, and His presence.

One of my very favorite parables is in Luke 15, the story of the Prodigal Son. Though the story is about a father's love for his lost son, it is really a picture of God the Father's love for you. God's love is looking for you, no matter how lost you feel. God's searching love can find you, no matter how many times you may have fallen into sin. God's hands of mercy are reaching out to pick you up and to love and forgive you.

Ladies and gentlemen, that's where you will find hope, and that's why I call Principle 2 the "hope" principle.

Hope

Let's look at what the word HOPE means in Principle 2:

Higher Power

Openness to change

Power to change

Expect to change

H stands for HIGHER power. Our Higher Power is the one and only true Higher Power and He has a name: Jesus Christ!

In the past you may have believed in Jesus' existence and you may have even attended church. But what you will find in Principle 2 is a personal relationship with Christ. You will see that Jesus desires a hands-on, day-to-day, moment-to-moment relationship with us. For He can do for us what we have never been able to do for ourselves. Romans 11:36 (TLB) says, "Everything comes from God alone. Everything lives by his power."

Many people today believe their doubts and doubt their beliefs! Have you ever seen an idea? Have you ever seen love? Have you ever seen faith? Of course not. You may have seen *acts* of faith and love, but the real things—the lasting things—in the world are the invisible spiritual realities.

This leads us to the first four words of the second step: "We came to believe . . ." Saying that we "came to believe" in anything describes a process. Belief is a result of consideration, doubt, reasoning, and concluding.

In 2 Corinthians 12:9 (PHILLIPS), Jesus tells us, "My grace is enough for you: for where there is weakness, my power is shown the more completely."

On page 1229 the *Life Recovery Bible* states, "The ability to form beliefs is the mark of God's image in our life. It leads to action."

The next letter in hope is *O*, which stands for OPENNESS to change.

What is the process that leads to solid belief, which leads you to change your life? Let's look at the first four words in Step 2 again: "We came to believe . . ."

- "We came . . ." We took the first step when we attended our first recovery meeting!

- "We came to . . ." We stopped denying our hurts, hang-ups, and habits!

- "We came to believe . . ." We started to believe and receive God's power to help us recover.

Hope is openness to change. Sometimes we are afraid to change, even if our past was painful. We resist change because of our fear of the unknown, or, in our despair, we think we don't deserve anything better.

Here's the good news: Hope opens doors where despair closes them! Hope discovers what can be done instead of grumbling about what can't be done.

Throughout your life you will continue to encounter hurts and trials that you are powerless to change, but with God's help you can be open to allow those circumstances and situations to change you—to make you better—not bitter.

Ephesians 4:23 (TLB) gives us a challenge to that end: "Now your attitudes and thoughts must all be constantly changing for the better. . . . You must be a new and different person."

How will you do that? The letter *P* tells us about POWER to change.

In the past, we may have wanted to change and were unable to do so; we could not free ourselves from our hurts, hang-ups, or habits. In Principle 2, we understand that God's power can change us and our situation. Philippians 4:13 (TLB) confirms it: "For I can do everything God asks me to with the help of Christ who gives me the strength and power."

Power to change comes from God's grace. You see, hope draws its power from a deep trust in God, like that of the psalmist, who wrote, "Lead me; teach me; for you are the God who gives me salvation. I have no hope except in you" (Psalm 25:5 TLB).

In Principle 2, we begin to understand that God's power can change us and our situation. And once we tap into that power, right actions—Christ-like actions—will follow naturally as by-products of working the principles and following the one and only Higher Power, Jesus Christ.

The last letter in hope is *E*: EXPECT to change.

Remember you are only at the second principle. *Don't quit before the miracle happens!* With God's help, the changes that you have longed for are just *steps* away. Philippians 1:6 (TLB) expresses my heart: "I am sure that God who began the good work within you will keep right on helping you grow in his grace until his task within you is finally finished on that day when Jesus Christ returns."

You know, you can't do anything unless you get started, so how much faith do you need to get started?

Matthew 17:20 tells us, "For if you had faith even as small as a tiny mustard seed you could say to this mountain, 'Move!' and it would go far away. Nothing would be impossible."

It's reassuring to know that you do not need large amounts of faith to begin the recovery process. You need only a small amount, "as small as a tiny mustard seed," to effect change, to begin to move your mountains of hurts, hang-ups, and habits.

Wrap-up

Eternal life does not begin with death; it begins with faith! Hebrews 11:1 tells us what faith is: "Faith is being sure of what we hope for and certain of what we do not see." Faith—even faith the size of a mustard seed so small you can hardly see it—is the avenue to salvation. You can't find salvation through intellectual understanding, gifts of money, good works, or attending church. No! The way to find salvation, is described in Romans 10:9: "If you confess with your mouth, 'Jesus is Lord,' and believe in your heart that God raised him from the dead, you will be saved."

Yes, all you need is just a little faith. If you will put the faith you have in Jesus, your life will be changed! You will find hope in the only Higher Power, Jesus Christ. His Spirit will come with supernatural power into your heart. It can happen to you! It happened to me!

Tonight I encourage you to take this step of hope. It will give you the courage to reach out and hold Christ's hand and face the present with confidence and the future with realistic expectancy.

Simply put, my life without Christ is a hopeless end; with Him it is an endless hope.

Sanity

Principle 2: Earnestly believe that God exists, that I matter to Him, and that He has the power to help me recover.

Happy are those who mourn, for they shall be comforted.

Step 2: We came to believe that a power greater than ourselves could restore us to sanity.

For it is God who works in you to will and to act according to his good purpose.

Philippians 2:13

Introduction

We spent our first month on Principle 1. We finally were able to face our denial and admit that we are powerless to control our tendency to do the wrong thing and that our lives had become unmanageable—out of control!

Now what do we need to do? How and where do we get the control? The answer is to take the second step on our journey of recovery.

The second step tells us that we have come to believe that a power greater than ourselves could restore us to sanity. "Wait a minute!" you're saying. "I spent an entire month hearing that to begin my recovery I had to face and admit my denial. Now you're telling me that I must be crazy? That I need to be restored to sanity? Give me a break!"

No, Step 2 isn't saying that you're crazy. Let me try to explain what the word "sanity" means in this step.

As a result of admitting our powerlessness in Principle 1, we can move from chaos to hope in Principle 2. We talked about that in our last teaching session. Hope comes when we believe that a power greater than ourselves, our Higher Power, Jesus Christ, can and will restore us! Jesus can provide that power where we were powerless over our addictions and compulsive behaviors. He alone can restore order and meaning to our lives. He alone can restore us to sanity.

Sanity

Insanity has been defined as "doing the same thing over and over again, expecting a different result each time."

Sanity has been defined as "wholeness of mind; making decisions based on the truth."

Jesus is the only Higher Power who offers the truth, the power, the way, and the life.

The following acrostic, using the word *sanity*, shows some of the gifts we receive when we believe that our true Higher Power, Jesus Christ has the power and will restore us to SANITY!

Strength
Acceptance
New Life
Integrity
Trust
Your Higher Power

The first letter is *S*, which stands for STRENGTH.

When we accept Jesus as our Higher Power, we receive strength to face the fears that, in the past, have caused us to fight, flee, or freeze. Now we can say, "God is our refuge and strength, an ever-present help in trouble. Therefore we will not fear" (Psalm 46:1) and "My mind and my body may grow weak, but God is my strength; he is all I ever need" (Psalm 73:26 GNB).

Relying on our own power, our own strength is what got us here in the first place. We believed we didn't need God's help, strength, or power. It's almost like we were disconnected from our true power source—God!

Choosing to allow my life to finally run on God's power—not my own limited power, weakness, helplessness, or sense of inferiority—has turned out to be my greatest strength. God came in where my helplessness began. And He will do the same for you!

The next letter, *A*, stands for ACCEPTANCE.

Romans 15:7 (GNB) says, "Accept one another, then, for the glory of God, as Christ has accepted you."

When we take Step 2, we learn to have realistic expectations of ourselves and others. We learn not to relate to others in the same old way, expecting a different response or result than they have given us time and time again. We begin to find the sanity we have been searching for. We remember to pray and ask God "to give us the courage to change the things we can and to accept the things we cannot change."

As our faith grows and we get to know our Higher Power better, it becomes easier for us to accept others as they really are, *not as we would have them be!*

With acceptance, however, comes responsibility. We stop placing all the blame on others for our past actions and hurts.

The next letter, *N*, stands for NEW life.

In the pit of our hurts, habits, and hang-ups, we were at our very bottom. We know the feelings expressed in 2 Corinthians 1:8–9 (TLB): "We were really crushed and overwhelmed, and feared we would never live through it. We felt we were doomed to die and saw how powerless we were to help ourselves; but that was good, for then we put everything into the hands of God."

The verse goes on to say, "God . . . alone could save us . . . and we expect him to do it again and again."

The penalty for our sins was paid in full by Jesus on the cross. The hope of a new life is freedom from our bondage! "When someone becomes a Christian he becomes a brand new person inside. He is not the same any more. A new life has begun!" (2 Corinthians 5:17 TLB).

The next benefit of this step is the *I* in sanity: INTEGRITY.

We gain integrity as we begin to follow through on our promises. Others start trusting what we say. The apostle John placed great value on integrity: "Nothing gives me greater joy than to hear that my children are following the way of truth" (3 John 4 NCV).

Remember, a half-truth is a whole lie, and a lie is the result of weakness and fear. Truth fears nothing—nothing but concealment! The truth often hurts. But it's the lie that leaves the scars.

A man or woman of integrity and courage is not afraid to tell the truth. And that courage comes from a power greater than ourselves—Jesus Christ, the way, the TRUTH, and the life.

The *T* in sanity stands for TRUST.

As we work Step 2, we begin to trust in our relationships with others and our Higher Power. "It is dangerous to be concerned with what others think of you, but if you trust the LORD, you are safe" (Proverbs 29:25 GNB).

As we "let go and let God" and admit that our lives are unmanageable and we are powerless do anything about it, we learn to trust ourselves and others. We begin to make real friends in recovery, in our groups, at the Solid Rock Cafe, and in church. These are not the mere acquaintances and the fair-weather friends we knew while we were active in our addictions and compulsions. In recovery you can find real friends, brothers and sisters in Christ, to walk beside you on your journey through the steps—friends whom you can trust, with whom you can share, with whom you can grow in Christ.

The last letter in our acrostic this evening is *Y:* YOUR Higher Power, Jesus Christ, loves you just the way you are! "While we were still sinners, Christ died for us" (Romans 5:8).

No matter what comes your way, together you and God can handle it! "And God is faithful; He will not let you be tempted beyond what you can bear. But when you are tempted, he will also provide a way out" (1 Corinthians 10:13). "Praise be to the LORD, to God our Savior, who daily bears our burdens" (Psalm 68:19).

When we accept Jesus Christ as our Higher Power and Savior, we are not only guaranteed eternal life, but we also have God's protection in time of trials. Nahum 1:7 says, "The LORD is good, a refuge in times of trouble. He cares for those who trust in him."

Wrap-up

Recovery is a *daily* program, and we need a power greater than ourselves—a Higher Power who will provide us with the strength, acceptance, new life, integrity, and trust to allow us to make sane decisions based on His truth!

And if you complete the next principle, Principle 3, your future will be blessed and secure! Matthew 6:34 (TLB) says, "So don't be anxious about tomorrow. God will take care of your tomorrow too. Live one day at a time."

Let's close in prayer.

> *Dear God, I have tried to "fix" and "control" my life's hurts, hang-ups, or habits all by myself. I admit that, by myself, I am powerless to change. I need to begin to believe and receive Your power to help me recover. You loved me enough to send Your Son to the cross to die for my sins. Help me be open to the hope that I can only find in Him. Please help me to start living my life one day at a time. In Jesus' name I pray, AMEN.*

PRINCIPLE 2 TESTIMONY

Hi, my name is Judy, an adult child of an alcoholic (ACA). I'm a Christian struggling with the effects of being raised in chaos. I'm the oldest child of a career Air Force officer, so I learned at a very young age not to become attached to anything, because good-byes hurt too much. I started building walls to keep others out.

I dearly loved my father, but he spent most of my childhood away from home, leaving my siblings and me in the care of a mother who raged and criticized. I grew up believing there was something wrong with me, not my family. Try as I would, I could never do anything to please my mother. Bigger and thicker walls went up.

My sister Jeri was born a year and a day after me. From the beginning, I felt in competition with my sister. My mother paired us one against the other. If Jeri and I did something wrong, I got punished because I was the oldest and should have known better. If Jeri did something wrong, I still got punished because I was older and should have kept her out of trouble. Talk about growing a codependent! If I cried, I was sent to my room and told not to come out until I had a smile on my face. So, I learned to wear a mask and never reveal the hurt inside.

I was super responsible by the time I was five; I had to be to survive. I learned never to ask for help, and I learned how to anticipate my mother's every mood. I even felt a duty to protect my younger brother and sisters from my mother's rage and to comfort them. I also had to deal with my guilt when I failed. But above all, we had to appear perfect to the outside world. My mother's favorite line when we were caught doing something wrong was "What will other people think?"

By the time I reached junior high, I was an angry young girl. But, of course, since proper young ladies do not get angry—especially in my mother's house—I learned to cry instead. My punishment now for crying was to write one hundred times "God helps those who help themselves." Her idea was to cure a crybaby, but I came away with the impression that God only helps perfect people, and I knew that wasn't me.

I didn't know much about God growing up; church was hit-and-miss in my family. Church attendance was about image rather than worship. We did say grace before dinner, but it was more a routine than a prayer. I remember singing "Jesus Loves Me" and "Jesus Loves the Little Children," but the words were just words to a song; they meant nothing to me. So by the time I hit high school my impression of God was a distant person who lived in heaven, with a Son, Jesus, who helped perfect people when He wasn't too busy.

When I was in the eighth grade, my dad was sent to Vietnam. That was the worst year of my life, because the one person who loved me left. And Daddy never came back. Oh, *Dad* returned a year later, but he had developed a severe alcohol problem. He was home, but he withdrew from the whole family. I took the rejection hard. I kept trying to figure out what I did wrong. My home life became a crazy cycle: the more my dad drank, the more my mother raged; and the more she raged, the more he drank.

When I was sixteen I discovered boys. I found out if you slept with them, they would tell you, "I love you" and hold you, and just for a while, that terrible ache inside would go away. By the time I reached my junior year, I was a straight-A student with a full-blown reputation.

That same year I found out my parents had "had" to get married because my mother was pregnant with me. No wonder my mother hated me and my dad drank so much, I thought, certain it was my fault. Not too much longer after that everything came to a head. My family life, the pressure to be perfect, and my sexual behavior was too much for me to handle and I tried to commit suicide. Praise God I wasn't perfect at that, but from then on I just went through the motions of living. I had learned my lessons well: don't talk, don't trust, don't feel. I created a fantasy based on magical thinking and "if onlys" to replace the reality of broken promises and dreams.

The summer before my senior year, I went to a church revival with a schoolmate and accepted Christ as my Savior. At least, I went forward and prayed the prayer because everyone else did. I was even baptized. I truly did believe things would change. They had to change! When my mother found out what I did, she exploded. She said I was going to hell for what I did. I was already baptized as a baby and what I did was unforgivable. Now I was convinced God would never help me.

But then Chris came into my life and I didn't need God. It didn't matter that he dated my sister before me. I was determined to succeed where my sister had failed.

But the star athlete had a slight character flaw: a violent temper. I was thrown across a classroom one day into a pile of desks. I went to the office for help but was told I shouldn't make up stories about decent people. I learned an important rule that day: people will believe an image over the truth.

I stayed with Chris, even though he beat me up two more times before graduation. After all, I believed it was my fault and if I could just be perfect, he wouldn't hit me anymore. Chris went to West Point and I went to William and Mary and after graduation we got married. On our wedding night he beat me severely because I wasn't a virgin. Frightened and alone I withdrew further into my shell. I couldn't go home to say I was wrong; what was left of my pride wouldn't let me. So I chose to step into the cycle most battered women exist in: if I try hard enough, then this insanity will stop. I took all responsibility for the violence in my marriage. My entire existence focused on pleasing Chris, who became my god.

As Chris's use of marijuana and alcohol increased, so did the violence. And it didn't stop at the verbal and physical level, but escalated to sexual abuse as well. I did try to escape once when my son, Jeff, was six months old (he's almost eighteen now). Chris came home and caught me trying to leave and I received the worst beating ever. As he beat my head into a wall with his hands around my throat, he said if I ever tried to leave again, no one would ever find me. Then he laughed and said, "Go ahead and tell. No one will ever believe you. I'm the perfect officer and a West Point grad. They will think you're crazy." So, I never left and I never told. I hid my bruises and hid my soul. I truly began to believe I was insane and God was punishing me for every guy I slept with. I believed I deserved what I was getting and, when I began to acknowledge that Chris was being unfaithful, it confirmed that I was worthless and unlovable. But, despite all the chaos—the alcohol, drugs, affairs, and violence—we were the perfect couple to the outside world. I had learned that image was everything, and I used every ounce of energy preserving it.

Our oldest son, Jeff, wasn't immune to the violence. He has memories of me being hit. Most of his memories, though, are the sounds of my pain and tears. He would hear the violence in the night and then wake to see Mommy's smiling face the next morning, looking as if nothing had happened. I'll be honest with you, I didn't know my son had all these memories. When Jeff was sixteen he was hospitalized for depression and suicide threats. The doctor asked me about Jeff's memories for confirmation. I thought he had been asleep; I thought I had somehow protected him. For his entire life, that was my focus: to love him with all my heart and protect him at all costs from the violence. All my love and protection helped contribute to the chaos in Jeff's life, though. I would inspect his room to make sure it was perfect. I would redo assignments and projects to make sure they were perfect. I made sure everything in our lives was up to Chris's standards. My motives were loving, but I taught my son, through my actions, that he could do nothing right.

In September of 1989, Jeff was diagnosed with diabetes. That same month, Chris's secretary was fired for being unprofessional when Chris broke off their affair to be with someone else in his company. It was too much for me to handle, and I actually got up the courage to ask Chris to leave. For once, things switched and I became powerful: he begged me not to kick him out. I know now he was desperate to preserve his image at the office, but at the time I thought he loved me and was sincere about recommitting. In January of 1990, Justin was conceived and I was truly happy for the first time in my life. It lasted for six months. During my sixth month of pregnancy, I found out Chris was involved with someone else. Because I was pregnant, he didn't hit me, but he raged until I was so upset I began having labor pains. Then he beat up Jeff. There I was again in the bottom of that familiar dark hold of chaos, only I wasn't alone; I'd brought the most precious things in the world with me—my boys.

So, I brought them into my world of isolation. We hid from the outside world and shut Chris out completely. I taught Jeff well how to shut down emotionally, to walk on egg shells, and not to trust or talk. He also learned to keep the image up at all cost. We were a strong partnership, mother and son; we had to be to survive. And into this mess, Justin joined us. He was everyone's focus because with Justin you could forget the chaos and pain for awhile and hold pure innocence.

When Justin was a year old, I heard about ACA. It took six months before I could get up the courage to go to a meeting. I remember a lot about that first meeting because it was so powerful. I walked in and was warmly welcomed; I didn't know how hungry I was for a smile. I heard the problem and solution read and realized this was where I belonged. Of course, I was under the impression that after a few quick meetings I would be cured. When people began sharing and I heard how long some of them had been in recovery, the hope of a quick fix vanished. What I remember most were the steps of recovery. And Step 2, "We came to believe that a power greater than ourselves could restore us to sanity." I decided to give God another chance—and that's all He needed to start working. I just had to believe a little.

As I got stronger, I confronted Chris with his affairs. I asked him to give up his current friend and go to counseling with me. We had sixteen years of marriage and two beautiful boys, and I had a willing heart to try for all our sakes. Chris did not and on April 21, 1992, he left the family for good. God has been working powerfully in my life since then. That first year, I discovered Saddleback through an old friend who just happened to call after Chris left. The first sermon I heard from Pastor Rick was "Why Isn't Life Fair?" I've been learning and growing through Saddleback since then. I found a wonderful therapist and survived the divorce process. I feel like I've been on God's fast track since I rededicated my life to Him. He brought me to Celebrate and I became an ACA group leader in February 1993. I began and graduated from a master's program in counseling psychology. I'm currently an MFCC intern with Lutheran Social Services. Life has not been perfect; it's been a long and difficult process of personal and family recovery.

Children are not immune to family violence, they learn from it. And last year, Jeff stepped into repeating the cycle. He threatened his girlfriend and she took out a restraining order on him. One day he walked by the store where she worked and landed in juvenile hall for two weeks. He learned well from his dad, and he thought he was immune from consequences. Praise God, Jeff's getting object lessons early in life; the consequences have been swift and hard. But he's learning—slowly—to undo the lessons of the past.

Each step of the way, God takes me to deeper levels of my fears and pains, helps me face them, and cleans out the wounds. He gifted me with the most wonderful accountability partner, who's been there to support and love me and let me be me. God gave me an ACA family where I get the nurturing and support I didn't get from my own family. They also provided a safe place where I could take off my mask and cry out my pain. He provided godly men in my life so I could learn all men are not jerks, and you can get safe hugs in a safe place with people who love you just because you're you. God provided an abundance for me because He knew the greatest storm of my life was still ahead—the one I am in the midst of now. I can look back over the last four years and see how He has prepared me for this storm. I've got a good strong boat, and He made sure I believed He would never leave or abandon me.

On Mother's Day last year, after he came home from a visit with his stepmother and dad, my younger son, Justin, disclosed that his dad had mistreated him. I panicked for a second but then went straight to God for His guidance. I've been through enough storms to know not to try and row the boat by myself. God led us to counseling which, in turn, led me to the current storm I'm churning in. Right now it appears to me as if all doors have been closed. Chris's image appears to be a powerful influence on everyone who speaks with him. There are times I feel I have already lost this case.

But, into my fears, God shined a candle. On January 31, at midweek service, Pastor Tom spoke about impossible situations. How God loves impossible situations because He uses them to stretch our faith, strengthen our hope, and to show His incredible love for us. My ACA group knows how I have been struggling with my faith and hope these past months. They know how I am fighting the magical thinking and broken promises of my youth in order to put total trust in God. He didn't lead me here to watch me fall now. People will do that to you. GOD DOESN'T! For me to stand before you today is a mighty leap of faith. I'd rather stay in the safety behind my walls and trust God there to help me work through my doubts and fears. When I was asked to do my testimony, I wanted to do Step 3. Actually, I wanted to wait until my storm was over and then share with you what God had done after the fact. But I was encouraged to share my hope and I realized what God was asking me to do. It's one thing to believe in your heart that God will deliver you, it's a bigger step of faith to say to those you trust, "I expect a miracle." I've been pushed out from behind the safety of my walls to proclaim my hope: my God is a God of impossible situations and I *do* expect a miracle. Romans 5:3–5 says, "We also rejoice in our sufferings, because we know that suffering produces perseverance; perseverance, character; and character, hope. And hope does not disappoint us, because God has poured out his love into our hearts by the Holy Spirit, whom he has given us."

As a friend always asks me when I start to get discouraged, "Judy Lynn, how big is your God?" He's big enough to free me from my fears of Chris, to tell the secrets of the past to, and to trust His light to shine on the truth and crush the false images. He knew the battle was coming. He prepared me for it, and He's providing His abundance during it. I do believe a power greater than myself can restore my family to sanity. My name is Judy, and I am overcoming the chaos of my past through Jesus Christ. Thanks for letting me share.

Principle 3

Consciously choose to commit all my life and will to Christ's care and control.

"Happy are the meek."

Turn

Principle 3: Consciously choose to commit all my life and will to Christ's care and control.

Happy are the meek.

Step 3: We made a decision to turn our lives and our wills over to the care of God.

Therefore, I urge you, brothers, in view of God's mercy, to offer your bodies as living sacrifices, holy and pleasing to God—this is your spiritual act of worship.

Romans 12:1

Principle 3 states that we choose to commit our *lives* and *wills* to Christ's care. Step 3 in AA's 12 Steps says "turn our *wills* and *lives*." I think Bill W., founder of Alcoholics Anonymous, got this step turned around. I believe that we must first commit and surrender our lives to the true Higher Power, Jesus Christ, and then we are able to turn over our wills to Him. Would you all agree with that?

When you choose to live this principle, you consciously choose to commit all your life and will to Christ's care and control.

How do you do that? How do you turn your life and will over to your Higher Power, Jesus Christ?

Turn

Let's look at tonight's acrostic for the answer to that question.

Trust

Understand

Repent

New life

This step ends with new life, but you must first take three actions before that life can be yours. You must trust, understand, and repent.

First let's talk about TRUST.

Have you ever been behind a semi-truck on a two-lane mountain road? Last summer Cheryl and I were taking Highway 1 toward Northern California. We were in the mountains and the scenery was beautiful. At one point, we approached a very steep incline and there must have been ten cars ahead of us. All of us were stuck behind a very slow-moving eighteen-wheeler.

The truck chugged very slowly up the hill. All of a sudden, the driver stuck his arm out of the window and motioned the cars to go around him. By his arm movement, he was telling us it was safe, there was no oncoming traffic ahead and we could pass him. One by one, the drivers of the cars trusted their own and their families' lives to a total stranger, as they moved out and in *blind trust* went around the slow truck.

All of the sudden, it hit me! Not the truck. No, I realized that we trust our lives to complete strangers every day. We trust that oncoming cars will stop at intersections. We trust that the hamburgers we eat at fast-food restaurants won't make us sick.

Why then is it so hard for us to trust our lives to the care of God, whose eye is always upon us? I don't know about you, but I would rather walk with God in the darkest valley than walk alone, or with a stranger, in the light.

In Principle 3, you make the one-time *decision* to turn your life over to the care of God. It's your choice, not chance, that determines your destiny. And that decision only requires trust, putting your faith into action!

But what is faith? Faith is *not* a sense, sight, or reason. Faith is simply taking God at His word! And God's Word tells us in Romans 10:9 (GNB): "If you declare with your lips, 'Jesus is Lord,' and believe in your heart that God raised him from the dead, you will be saved."

For some people that's just way too simple. They want to make salvation much more difficult. But it isn't! Our salvation, thank God, depends on God's love for us, not our love for Him.

After you have decided to trust, the next step is to UNDERSTAND. Relying solely on our own understanding got most of us into recovery in the first place! After you make the decision to ask Jesus into your life, you need to begin to seek His will for your life in all your decisions. You need to get to know and understand Him and what He wants for your life.

Proverbs 3:5–6 says, "Trust in the LORD with all your heart and lean not on your own understanding; in all your ways acknowledge him, and he will make your paths straight. "

You see, our understanding is earthbound. It's human to the core. Limited. Finite. We operate in a dimension totally unlike that of our Lord. He knows no such limitations. We see now; God sees forever!

You know something really strange? It has taken me all my life to understand that it is not necessary for me to understand everything.

First Corinthians 13:9–13 (GNB) tells us, "For our gifts of knowledge . . . are only partial; but when what is perfect comes, then what is partial will disappear. . . . What we see now is like the dim image in a mirror; then we shall see face to face. What I know now is only partial; then it will be complete, as complete as God's knowledge of me."

Someday we will see Jesus face-to-face. The fog of interpretation will be lifted, and our understanding will be perfected.

Praise God that we do not need a perfect understanding of Him to ask Jesus into our lives as our Lord and Savior. Why? Because God does not lead you year by year. Not even day by day. God directs your way step by step.

The third letter in our acrostic, *R*, stands for REPENT.

Some people repent of their sins by thanking the Lord that they aren't half as bad as their neighbors. That's not true repentance! Repentance is how you begin to enjoy the freedom of your loving relationship with God. True repentance affects our whole person and changes our entire view of life. Repentance is to take God's point of view on our lives instead of our own.

To truly repent you need to do two things: First, turn away from your sins; second, turn toward God. The Bible has much to say about repentence:

"Turn from your sins and act on this glorious news!" (Mark 1:15 TLB).

"Repent! Turn away from all your offenses; then sin will not be your downfall. Rid yourselves of all the offenses you have committed, and get a new heart and a new spirit" (Ezekiel 18:30–31).

"Don't let the world around you squeeze you into its own mold, but let God remake you so that your whole attitude of mind is changed" (Romans 12:2 PHILLIPS).

It seems that most people repent of their sins more from a fear of punishment than from a real change of heart. But repentance is not self-loathing; it is God-loving. God isn't looking forward to punishing you! He is eagerly anticipating with open arms your turning toward Him. Then when you have chosen to turn from your sin toward Him, He will joyously give to you what the last letter in tonight's acrostic stands for: NEW life.

The new life that you will receive is the result of taking the three actions that we just covered: trusting, understanding, and repenting.

As a pastor, I have heard some pretty glum definitions of life. These are just a few:

"Life is a hereditary disease."

"Life is a sentence that we have to serve for being born."

"Life is a predicament that precedes death."

"Life's a tough proposition; and the first hundred years are the hardest."

Those are depressing words that you may feel are true if your life doesn't include Jesus Christ. After you ask Jesus into your heart, you will have a new life! You will no longer be bound to your old sinful nature. You will receive a new loving nature dwelling within you from Christ.

God has declared you "not guilty," and you no longer have to live under the power of sin! Romans 3:22 (TLB) says it well: "Now God says he will accept and acquit us—declare us 'not guilty'—if we trust Jesus Christ to take away our sins."

Second Corinthians 5:17 (GNB) says: "When anyone is joined in Christ he is a new being; the old is gone, the new has come."

In what ways does the "new life" demonstrate itself in us?

The "old you" said,	The "new you" says,
Save your life!	You must lose your life to keep it (Mark 8:35).
Get, get, get!	Give and it will be given to you (Luke 6:38).
Lead, at all costs.	Serve (John 13:12).
Lie; the truth only complicates things.	Speak the truth in love (Ephesians 4:29).
Hate your enemy.	Love your enemy (Matthew 5:44).

Let's wrap this up now.

Wrap-up

Again, the "turn" in Principle 3 includes three very important actions that lead to a new life in Christ: trusting, understanding, repenting.

The good news is, turning your life over to Christ is a once-in-a-lifetime commitment. Once you accept Christ in your life, it's a done deal. Ephesians 1:13 says your salvation is "sealed." You can't lose it! It's guaranteed by the Holy Spirit.

The rest of the principle, however, turning your *will* over to Him, requires daily recommitment! You can begin by going to your Bible regularly, opening it prayerfully, reading it expectantly, and living it joyfully!

If you haven't asked Jesus Christ to be your Higher Power, the Lord and Savior of your life, I encourage you to do so this evening. What are you waiting for? Pray this prayer.

Dear God, I have tried to do it all by myself on my own power, and I have failed. Today I want to turn my life over to You. I ask You to be my Lord and my Savior. You are the One and only Higher Power! I ask that You help me think less about me and my will. I want to daily turn my will over to You, to daily seek Your direction and wisdom for my life. Please continue to help me overcome my hurts, hang-ups, and habits, that victory over them may help others as they see Your power at work in changing my life. Help me to do Your will always. In Jesus' name I pray, AMEN.

Lesson 6

Action

Principle 3: Consciously choose to commit all my life and will to Christ's care and control.

Happy are the meek.

Step 3: We made a decision to turn our lives and our wills over to the care of God.

Therefore, I urge you, brothers, in view of God's mercy, to offer your bodies as living sacrifices, holy and pleasing to God—this is your spiritual act of worship.

Romans 12:1

Introduction

When we get to Principle 3, we have worked, with God's help, the first two principles to the best of our ability. We admitted our lives were out of control and unmanageable, and we came to believe that God could restore us.

But even after taking the first two steps we can still be stuck in the *cycle of failure* that keeps us bound by guilt, anger, fear, and depression.

Tonight we are going to see how to get "unstuck."

How do we get past those old familiar negative barriers of pride, fear, guilt, worry, and doubt—those barriers that keep us from taking this step? The answer is *action!*

Principle 3 is all about ACTION. It states: "We choose to commit …" Making a choice requires action.

Almost everyone knows the difference between right and wrong, but most people don't like making decisions. We just follow the crowd because it's easier than making the decision to do what we know is right. We procrastinate making commitments that will allow change to occur from the pain of our hurts, hang-ups, and habits.

Do you know that some people think that deciding whether or not to discard their old toothbrush is a major decision? Others are so indecisive that their favorite color is plaid!

But seriously, do you know that to not decide is to decide?

Do you know putting off the decision to accept Jesus Christ as your Higher Power, Lord, and Savior really is making the decision *not to accept Him*?

Principle 3 is like opening the door: All you need is the willingness to make the decision. Christ will do the rest!

He said, "Here I am! I stand at the door and knock. If anyone hears my voice and opens the door, I will come in and eat with him, and he with me" (Revelation 3:20).

Action

Let's look at tonight's acrostic: ACTION.

Accept

Commit

Turn it over

It's only the beginning

One day at a time

Next step

The first letter, *A,* stands for **ACCEPT** Jesus Christ as your Higher Power and Savior!

Make the once-in-a-lifetime *decision* to ask Jesus into your heart. Make the decision to establish that personal relationship with your Higher Power that He so desires. Now is the time to choose to commit your life. God is saying make it today! Satan says do it tomorrow.

In Romans 10:9 (GNB) God's Word tells us, "If you declare with your lips, 'Jesus is Lord,' and believe in your heart that God raised him from the dead, you will be saved."

It's only after you make this decision that you can begin to COMMIT to start asking and following *His* will! That's the *C* of the word action.

I would venture that all of us here tonight have tried to run our lives on our own power and will and found it to be less than successful. In Principle 3, we change our definition of willpower. Willpower becomes the willingness to accept God's power to guide your life. We come to see that there is no room for God if we are full of ourselves.

We need to pray the prayer the psalmist prayed when he said, "Teach me to do your will, for you are my God; may your good Spirit lead me on level ground" (Psalm 143:10).

The letter *T* in action stands for TURN it over.

"Let go and let God." You have heard that phase many times in recovery. It doesn't say just let go of some things to God. It doesn't say just let go of, turn over, only the *big* things.

Proverbs 3:6 (TLB) tells us, "In *everything* you do, put God first, and he will direct you and crown your efforts with success."

"In *everything* you do." Not just the big things, not just the little things. Everything! You see, Jesus Christ just doesn't want a relationship with part of you. He desires a relationship with *all* of you.

What burdens are you carrying tonight that you want to turn over to Jesus? He says, "Come to me and I will give you rest—all of you who work so hard beneath a heavy yoke. Wear my yoke—for it fits perfectly—and let me teach you; for I am gentle and humble, and you shall find rest for your souls; for I give you only light burdens" (Matthew 11:28–30 TLB).

The next letter in action is *I*. IT'S only the beginning.

In the third principle we make the initial decision to accept Christ as our personal Savior. Then we can make the commitment to seek and follow

God's will. The new life that begins with this decision is followed by a life-long process of growing as a Christian.

Philippians 1:6 (TLB) puts it this way: "God who began the good work within you will keep right on helping you grow in his grace until his task within you is finally finished."

I like to compare the third principle to buying a new house. First you make the decision to buy the new house. But that's only the beginning. There are still more steps that you need to take before you actually can move into the house. You need to go to the bank and apply for the loan. You need to get an appraisal. You need to complete the escrow. You need to contact the moving company. You need to contact the utility companies—all before you are ready to move in.

Recovery is not a three-principle program! Principle 3 is only the exciting beginning of a new life—a life we live in a new way: ONE day at a time.

Our recoveries happen one day at a time. If we remain stuck in the yesterday or constantly worry about tomorrow, we will waste the precious time of the present. And it is only in the present that change and growth can occur. We can't change yesterday and we can only pray for tomorrow. Jesus gave us instructions for living this philosophy: "Don't be anxious about tomorrow. God will take care of your tomorrow too. Live one day at a time" (Matthew 6:34 TLB).

Believe me, if I could go back and change the past, I would do many things differently. I would choose to spare my family the pain and the hurt that my alcoholism caused. But I can't change even one thing that happened in my past. And neither can you.

And on the other side of the coin, I can't live somewhere way off in the future, always worrying if "this or that" is going to happen. And neither can you. I leave that up to God.

But I can and do live in today! And I can, with Jesus Christ's guidance and direction, make a difference in the way I live today. And so can you. You can make a difference one day at a time.

Wrap-up

This, finally brings us to the last letter in our acrostic. *N* stands for NEXT step.

The next step is to ask Jesus into your life to be your Higher Power. How? It's very simple.

Pastor Rick Warren has developed an easy way for you to establish a "spiritual B.A.S.E." for your life. Ask yourself the following four questions, and if you answer yes to all of them, pray the prayer that follows. That's it. That's all you have to do!

Do I

- **B**elieve Jesus Christ died on the cross for me and showed He was God by coming back to life? (1 Corinthians 15:2–4)

- **A**ccept God's free forgiveness for my sins? (Romans 3:22)

- **S**witch to God's plan for my life? (Mark 1:16; Romans 12:2)

- **E**xpress my desire for Christ to be the director of my life? (Romans 10:9)

If you are ready to take this step, in a minute, we will pray together. If you have already taken this step, use this prayer to recommit to continue to seek and follow God's will.

Dear God, there are some here this evening that need to make the decision to commit their lives into Your hands, to ask You into their hearts as their Lord and Savior. Give them the courage to silently do so right now in this moment. It is the most important decision that they will ever make.

Pray with me. I'll say a phrase and you repeat it in your heart.

Dear God, I believe You sent your Son, Jesus, to die for my sins so I can be forgiven. I'm sorry for my sins, and I want to live the rest of my life the way You want me to. Please put Your Spirit in my life to direct me, AMEN.

If you made the decision to invite Christ into your life, let someone know. I would love to talk to you after our fellowship time.

PRINCIPLE 3 TESTIMONY

My name is Brenda, and my story begins in the south—Louisville, Kentucky, to be exact—where I was born into an all-white family. Kind of like the movie *The Jerk,* where Steve Martin says, "I was born a poor black child," except mine was just the opposite: I was born a poor "white child." It was funny in the movie, but not in my life.

I guess you are wondering how this could be. Well, my mother was married and had one child, my older brother. She worked at distilling (Kentucky being the whiskey capital of the world), and as she was leaving work one night, she got into an elevator and was attacked, beaten, and raped by a black man. As God would have it (I know this now), I was the result of this incident.

I've wondered more times than you can imagine why my mom didn't give me up, since in the south all those years ago, a black and white relationship was more than a no-no. This story is not about prejudice, but it was so prevalent in those days, especially in the south, and particularly among uneducated people. So certainly my mother realized that my birth into this white family was going to more than complicate things for her and definitely for me.

I was hated from the very beginning by the man to whom my mom was married. He mistreated me from the start. By the time I was in the first grade I had been beaten or hit daily. I had been burned, had knives thrown at me that split my nose right down the middle, was scalded by soup, locked in closets, and was literally stomped on until I lost all bodily function (that was because I couldn't memorize a song). I was made to get up at 3:00 A.M. to go put cigarettes up in a tree so this man could shoot them out, and he would often shoot before I was out of the tree. And of course I was sexually abused as well. He was a very sick man. You see, he was an alcoholic, and he died when I was in the first grade.

My mom proceeded to meet alcoholic after alcoholic, get involved and have a child. Each one would abuse her and us and then move on. She then got involved with another wrong crowd and wound up in prison. We were sent to live with a grandmother who was cordial enough and did what she was supposed to do and take care of us while Mom was away, but she was not very affectionate.

Then there were the other relatives, the uncles and the cousins that pretty much left the other kids alone—all but me. I was the target for much more mental, physical, and sexual abuse by them all. In fact, I used to think I had a sign painted on me that said, "Pick on me," or "Kick me," or "Hit me," or "Here I am," because that's all I ever got. There was no love; there were no kind words, no words of encouragement, and no terms of endearment.

Well, needless to say, I grew up very, very tough. I had to fight my way through every situation, constantly defending myself. I didn't have many friends in school, really, because the kids weren't allowed to hang out with a "black girl." I was the only black kid in all my schooling through graduation, truly the odd man out.

I do have to tell you, I really liked going to school. It was about the safest place I could be. Any place was better than home. In fact, I left home at fourteen but found it really rough, so I had to return to the insanity.

Anyway, in school I became very involved in sports—track was my forte—and I was voted "Most Athletic" in my senior year. But not once did one person from that family come to see me run. Not once.

Since so many people had hated me instantly because of my color, I remember thinking when I was quite young that one day I just wasn't going to accept people not liking me, unless they gave me a chance first! Just give me five minutes. If you don't like me, okay, but please give me a chance.

I wanted so much to be like the other kids and do normal things—go skating, go to dances, and such—but it just wasn't going to happen because no one wanted or could take a "black girl" anywhere except, that is, behind closed doors, so I proceeded, as they say, to "look for love in all the wrong places." I found a group of undesirables like myself that I could be a part of. This took place in the 70s, the biggest drug era ever. Believe me when I tell you that I have tried them all. I went on to what I call my mode of self-destruction. I met a guy, got pregnant, and had a son. I can tell you for sure, my son has been my lifesaver. There's no doubt that God sent him to me.

I have always been blessed and been able to have a job or two. In fact, I had three jobs when I bought my first house at age thirty-three. I moved into that house, became a drug dealer, and was still taking care of business. I was what you would call a high-functioning drug addict. I always had a job, a car, great clothes, and money. How could I possibly have a problem?

A few years later, I moved to Houston. It was there that I became involved in cocaine. I was stopped for a traffic violation, was searched, and they found a one-pound bag in my purse (because at this time I was doing probably close to an eighth a day). I was put on probation, and drug testing was a part of it. I tried beating the system by drinking pickle juice. (Don't try it; it doesn't work.) Anyway, I was sent to jail for three months for breaking probation. Talk about a wake-up call! Don't think I changed instantly, but I knew then that this was not how I was going to live.

I had always been close to my mom, and I know that she protected me to the best of her ability. She was the one person who loved me and who I trusted. The day after I got out of jail, my mom passed away. I was crushed: the one person I could trust was gone.

I packed up everything and moved from Houston to California. I had to have my probation and counseling transferred, and I continued to stay in a program.

After meeting a man here who turned out to be an abuser (I wasn't allowed to go out of the house except for work and groceries), I found myself watching Fred Price on the TV. Through him, God spoke to me as loudly as I'm speaking to you now. I'm sure that He was speaking directly to me. He had a lot to say Sunday after Sunday, once He got my attention.

I prayed to God and asked Him to get me out of this relationship and sure enough, six months later, I was free. I started attending another church and gave my life to the Lord two weeks before New Year's Day.

Then, on New Year's Day, I was raped. There were a few things that had stuck with me in my Christian life, and one was that "all good things are from above," so I still believe that incident was a swipe at me from Satan (certainly not his last) because he didn't want to lose me as one of his warriors.

I know that God has had a plan for me all along. I believe that part of His plan was for me to start on my recovery then and there. I had been pushing all those feelings, all those ugly things that had happened to me as a child, into a "Pandora's box."

Once on my road to recovery, I discovered that I had to open up that box. I had to take each item out and face it, one item at a time. I'm not going to tell you that it was easy, because it wasn't. It was as painful the second time around as it was the first, but I made the most fascinating discovery: Regardless of all those things people had done to me as a child and throughout life, and even the acting out that I had done, I was not guilty. It was not my fault. I really and truly was not the terrible, horrible person that I thought and felt that I was. In fact, I can stand here today and tell you that God has let me see that I really am not a bad person at all.

As I have had the opportunity to read God's Word, I can see that my life as it was, was part of God's plan from the beginning, not to hurt me by any means, but to shape me and to mold me into the person I am today.

After having been in therapy and in a program for a few years and also being a Christian, I knew that all that insanity had been removed from my life. It was then that I started praying for a man to be with—one who God would send me. A few months later I met the man who would soon become my husband. He was a fun-loving guy who was a Christian and loved the Lord.

After a short period of time, we were married. We were blessed twenty-fold from the beginning. God poured His blessings out on us, gave us a beautiful house on the lake, great cars, a hair salon. God was good.

After about eight months, my husband started behaving differently—drinking a lot and being gone for three to four days at a time. As the months went on, I discovered that I had, in fact, married an addict.

It was at this time that some friends had invited us to Saddleback to hear their kids sing in the Christmas program. We were looking for a church home at the time and never felt the need to be anywhere but here at Saddleback after that night.

During some of the tough times when my husband was acting out, I discovered Celebrate Recovery. I encouraged him to come with me, and he did a few times but rarely stayed for the groups.

Anyway, I finally had to make the decision for me—since I am the only one I'm in charge of—to come and commit myself to the program. I desperately needed to talk to someone. The problem I had at the time was deciding which group to go to, since I needed them all. I chose co-dependents in a chemically addicted relationship.

My husband's disease was progressing at such a rate that I could not keep up with it. Needless to say, our marriage was suffering, but I kept on praying and asking for prayer, and I kept on trusting God for all of the answers.

After about three months, I was asked to lead the group, which I did with God's help all the way to January of 1995.

It is here that the third principle comes in: Consciously choose to commit all my life and will to Christ's care.

Second Samuel 22:2–3 (TLB) says, "Jehovah is my Rock, my fortress and my Savior. He is my shield and my salvation, my refuge and high tower."

It is to my complete and utter amazement that I stand before you all tonight to be able to give praise to God. You see, if it were up to Satan, I would have died last January, when my husband attacked and beat me and left me unconscious. It is due to the God that I serve and the name of Jesus Christ, however, that I am here, and I want to give Him all of the glory.

As I recap the events of that day and all those long months that followed, I must tell you that God is real and I have seen His face! After I was beaten and knocked unconscious, my car was stolen. My purse, my money, credit cards, jewelry, and everything else that I considered valuable at that time were also taken. I even had to leave my beautiful home that I loved so much. I left that day for the hospital with just a bag of clothes, my broken body and spirit, and my Bible. I thought that everything was gone. This is when some miracles started taking place, and not just one.

First of all, God sent Jesus Christ to me during the attack to ward off Satan so I could escape. After that traumatic experience, God totally surrounded me with angels on earth. One was a girlfriend from work who soothed me with her voice, took me to the hospital, and got me some food and a hotel for the night. She also canceled all of my credit cards and my bank account.

Next was another girlfriend (adopted by missionaries in Africa) from my job who came to get me from the hotel. She gave me a car to drive and the keys to her apartment, which was a very safe place to be. She also gave me a purse (ha! ha!) even though all I had to put in it was my Bible. What else did I need?

I had to take a week off work due to bruises to my body and my ego. I didn't return to my house until three weeks later, which is when another miracle took place. I had been so ashamed of what had happened to me, yet I knew that I had to make an emergency move of out my house. Finally, the day before I moved, I made two phone calls to people in the choir, and I also mentioned my situation to a couple of people at my Celebrate rehearsal. I was completely shocked when, at 9:00 on Saturday morning, seventeen people showed up on my doorstep. Eight women started packing like bandits. The men put the things in the truck, and my whole house was in storage by 1:00 that afternoon. Talk about a miracle! Only God could have done that job. I was even able to go to church that night. Then three weeks later I moved again, and everyone was there again.

As I think about it, there was not a day that went by last year without some trial in it of some sort. I had to deal with the closing of the house and the bank accounts, the lease people, the police and detectives, lawyers, and of course, I still had to work and perform at a job that was sometimes highly stressful.

I finally got my car back from an impound lot three weeks later. By the grace of God and my guardian angel, there was not a scratch on it. All of my stereo equipment was gone out of it, which turned out to be a blessing in disguise. You see, in all that quiet time in the car, God and I had a lot of wonderful, loving conversations. We had more quiet time than we had ever had before.

I was trying to manage my townhouse and the hair salon and all of the overhead that goes with it. I couldn't do it, so God did. The lease was up on the business in August, and with the help of my all-girls' Celebrate wrecking team, we took that shop apart and closed those doors. God always made a way where there seemed to be no way!

Every time there was something going on up here at church, I was one of the first to arrive. I was here Tuesday for both rehearsals, Wednesday for midweek service, and I sang on Thursday night at Women's Bible Study. Of course, I was here on Fridays, and if the choir sang, I was here on Saturday and Sunday.

I needed this church and my church family to help me stand in the midst of it all. God has been so faithful to me. As it turned out, I had the best year financially that I've ever had at my job, and God just blessed me with a new house. Did I say I thought I had lost everything? I think not! I have gained more through my trials than I could have ever lost! Just to have seen God's face was more than I could ever have asked for.

In looking at this last year, I see that I can now better accept the things I cannot change, and it truly takes courage to change the things you can, and I have struggled with the wisdom to know the difference.

I would like to tell you that my marriage survived and is flourishing. I am sorry to say that it is not. Our divorce was final in January of this year. I'm trusting God to see me through this time as well. He has promised me that He will never leave me or forsake me. Brothers and sisters, the same holds true for you. Just ask Him.

In 2 Corinthians 4:8 it says, "We are hard pressed on every side, but not crushed; perplexed, but not in despair; persecuted, but not abandoned; struck down, but not destroyed." Psalm 147:3 (KJV) says, "He healeth the broken in heart, and bindeth up their wounds." And Romans 8:28 says, "And we know that in all things God works for the good of those who love him, who have been called according to his purpose."

Thank you for letting me share!

Principle 4

Openly examine and confess my faults to myself,
to God, and to someone I trust.

"Happy are the pure in heart."

Moral

Principle 4: Openly examine and confess my faults to myself, to God, and to someone I trust.

Happy are the pure in heart.

Step 4: We made a searching and fearless moral inventory of ourselves.

Let us examine our ways and test them, and let us return to the Lord.
Lamentations 3:40

Introduction

Tonight we are going to really dig in and begin the growth process of recovery. Now, even though Principle 4 may bring some growing pains with it, tonight we are going to look at ways to maximize the growth and minimize the pain.

I wish I could say that you can escape the pain of your past altogether by going around it or jumping over it. But the only way I know to get rid of the pain of your past is to go through it. It has been said that "we need to use our past as a springboard, not a sofa—a guidepost, not a hitching post."

I know some people who spend their lives rationalizing the past, complaining about the present, and fearing the future. They, of course, are not moving down the road to recovery. By coming tonight, however, you have chosen to continue going forward. And if you choose to embark on the adventure of self-discovery that begins with Principle 4 and continues through Principle 5, I can guarantee you that growth will occur.

Principle 4 begins the process of "coming clean." Pastor Rick Warren calls this "truth decay." It is here that we openly examine and confess our faults to ourselves, to God, and another person we trust. We chip away and clean out all the decay of the past that has built up over the years and has kept us from really seeing the truth about our past and present situations.

A Moral Inventory

You may be wondering, "How do I do this thing called a moral inventory?"

That word "moral" scares some people. It scared me when I first worked this step in AA. Really, the word "moral" simply means honest!

In this step, you need to list, or inventory, all the significant events—good and bad—in your life. You need to be as honest as you can be to allow God to show you your part in each event and how that affected you and others.

Tonight's acrostic will explain the five things you need to do to make a MORAL inventory.

Make time

Open

Rely

Analyze

List

First you need to MAKE time. Schedule an appointment with yourself. Set aside a day or a weekend and get alone with God! God tells us in Job 33:33 (TLB): "Listen to me. Keep silence and I will teach you wisdom!"

The next letter in MORAL, *O,* stands for OPEN.

Remember when, as a child, you would visit the doctor, and he would say, "Open wide!" in that funny sing-song voice? Well, you need to "open wide" your heart and mind to allow the feelings that the pain of the past has blocked or caused you to deny. Denial may have protected you from your feelings and repressed your pain for awhile. But now it has also blocked and prevented your recovery from your hurts, hang-ups, and habits. You need to "open wide" to see the real truth.

Once you have seen the truth, you need to express it. Here's what Job had to say about being open: "Let me express my anguish. Let me be free to speak out of the bitterness of my soul" (7:11 TLB). Perhaps the following questions will help to "wake up" your feelings and get you started on your inventory!

Ask yourself, *What do I feel guilty about?* The first thing that came to your mind is what you need to address first in your inventory.

Do you know and understand the God-given purpose of guilt? God uses guilt to correct us through His Spirit when we are wrong. That's called conviction. And conviction hurts!

Now don't confuse conviction with condemnation. Romans 8:1 tells us, "There is now no condemnation for those who are in Christ." Once we have made the decision to ask Jesus into our hearts, once we confess our wrongs, accept Christ's perfect forgiveness, and turn from our sins, as far as God is concerned, guilt's purpose—to make us feel bad about what we did in the past—is finished. But we like to hold on to it and beat ourselves over the head—repeatedly—with it!

That's condemnation. But it's not from God, it's from ourselves. Principle 4 will help you let go of your guilt, once and for all.

The next question you need to ask is *What do I resent?*

Resentment results from burying our hurts. If resentments are then suppressed, left to decay, they cause anger, frustration, and depression. What we don't talk out creatively, we act out destructively.

Another big question that you need to openly ask during this step is *What are my fears?*

Personally, I have a fear of going to the dentist. But even though it may hurt while I'm in the chair, when he's done driving the decay away, I feel a lot better.

Fear prevents us from expressing ourselves honestly and taking an honest moral inventory. Joshua 1:9 (GNB) tells us, "Do not be afraid or discouraged, for I, the LORD your God, am with you wherever you go."

Next on the list of hard questions to ask yourself: *Am I trapped in self-pity, alibis, and/or dishonest thinking?* Remember, the truth does not change; your feelings do!

These questions are only the beginning of your inventory, but don't get discouraged. The next letter offers a reminder that you don't have to face this task alone.

The next letter is *R*, which stands for RELY.

Rely on Jesus to give you the courage and strength this step requires. Here's a suggestion: When your knees are knocking, it might help to kneel on them.

Isaiah 40:29 tells us that Jesus "gives strength to the weary and increases the power of the weak." You *can* do this with His help.

Before we go any farther, I want to remind you that the principles and steps are in order for a reason other than if they were listed a different way we wouldn't have a nifty acrostic! You need to complete Principle 3—turning your life and your will over to God—before you can successfully work Principle 4.

Once you know the love and power of the one and only Higher Power, Jesus Christ, there is no longer any need to fear this principle. Psalm 31:23–24 (TLB) tells us: "Oh, love the Lord, all of you who are his people; for the Lord protects those who are loyal to him. . . . So cheer up! Take courage if you are depending on the Lord." And remember, courage is not the absence of fear but the conquering of it.

Now you are ready to ANALYZE your past honestly.

To do a "searching and fearless" inventory, you must step out of your denial, because we cannot put our faults behind us until we face them. You must look through your denial of the past into the truth of the present— your true feelings, motives, thoughts, and, as in the *Star Wars* movie Obi-Wan Kenobi says, your "dark side."

Proverbs 20:27 (GNB) says, "The LORD gave us mind and conscience; we cannot hide from ourselves." Believe me, I know! I tried! My grandma used to tell me, "Johnny, it's not enough to be as honest as the day is long. You should behave yourself at night too!"

Some of you heard the word "analyze" and got fired up, because you love to pick apart the details of a situation and look at events from all angles. Others of you have broken out into a cold sweat at the thought of analyzing anything! For those of you whose hearts are pounding and whose palms are clammy, listen closely as we talk about the *L* in moral: LIST.

Your inventory is basically a written list of the events of your past—both good and bad. (Balance is important.) Seeing your past in print brings you face-to-face with the reality of your character defects. Your inventory becomes a black-and-white discovery of who you truly are way down deep.

But if you just look at all the *bad* things of your past, you will distort your inventory and open yourself to unnecessary pain. Lamentations 3:40 tells us, "Let us examine our ways and test them." The verse doesn't say, "just examine your bad, negative ways." You need to honestly focus on the "pros" and the "cons" of your past!

I know people who have neglected to balance their inventory and have gotten stuck in their recoveries. Or even worse, they judged the program to be too hard and too painful and stopped their journey of recovery altogether—and they slipped back to their old hurts, hang-ups, and habits of the past.

An important word of caution: Do not begin this step without a sponsor or a strong accountability partner! You need someone you trust to help keep you balanced during this step, not to do the work for you. Nobody can do that except you. But you need encouragement from someone who will support your progress and to share your pain. That's what this program is all about.

In two weeks we will look at how to find a sponsor. That's Lesson 8 in Participant's Guide 2. It will show you some of the qualities to look for in a sponsor, what the job of a sponsor is, and some suggestions on how to find a sponsor or an accountability partner. A great place to start is at Celebrate Recovery's Bar-B-Que next Friday night at 6:00. Then again, why wait? Start looking at the Solid Rock Cafe tonight at 9:00. That's how you begin Principle 4.

Wrap-up

At the information table, you will find some blank Principle 4 worksheets. In a few weeks, we will be talking about how to put them to use in helping you work this key step.

I encourage you to get Participant's Guide 2 tonight if you have completed Principle 3.

Start working Principle 4. What are you waiting for? Start working this program in earnest.

If you are new to recovery or this is your first recovery meeting, we are glad that you are here. Pick up the first participant's guide, *Stepping Out of Denial Into God's Grace,* and start this amazing journey with Jesus Christ. A healing journey that will lead you to freedom and truth. And by listening during the next two months, when you are ready to begin Principle 4, you will have a head start. You will also have a great understanding of the importance of Principle 4.

Let's pray.

Dear God, You know our past, all the good and the bad things that we've done. In this principle, we ask that You give us the strength and the courage to list them so that we can "come clean" and face them and the truth. Please help us reach out to others that You have placed along our "road to recovery." Thank You for providing them to help us keep balanced as we do our inventories. In Christ's name I pray, AMEN.

Sponsor

Principle 4: Openly examine and confess my faults to myself, to God, and to someone I trust.

Happy are the pure in heart.

Step 4: We made a searching and fearless moral inventory of ourselves.

Let us examine our ways and test them, and let us return to the LORD.
                                                                    Lamentations 3:40

Introduction

Last month, we talked about the importance of having a personal relationship with Jesus Christ, which you found when you made the decision to turn your life and your will over to the care of God.

Now you will see that the road to recovery is not meant to be traveled alone. You will find that you actually need three relationships. Most important is a relationship with Jesus Christ. In addition, you need the relationship of your recovery group or a church family. Last, you need the relationship of a sponsor and/or accountability partner. Identifying a sponsor is especially important before you begin Principles 4 through 6, in which you work on getting right with God, yourself, and others.

We talked two weeks ago about doing a moral inventory—your evaluation of your weaknesses (shortcomings) and strengths. It has been said that to attempt an inventory by yourself can be as futile as peeling an onion to find the core. When you're finished, there is nothing left but peelings and the tears.

As I said in Lesson 7, Principle 4 is all about getting rid of our "truth decay," about coming clean! Proverbs 15:14 tells us, "A wise person is hungry for the truth, while a fool feeds on trash." Are you ready to feed on the truth about your life? Well then, it's time to take out the trash!

That trash can get pretty heavy at times, so I don't want you to handle it alone. You need a genuine mentor, coach, or, in recovery terms, a sponsor. Some of you may still be unconvinced that you really need this person known as a sponsor, so tonight we are going to answer the five following questions:

1. Why do I need a sponsor?

2. What are the qualities of a sponsor?

3. What does a sponsor do?

4. How do I find a sponsor?

5. What is the difference between a sponsor and an accountability partner?

Why Do I Need a Sponsor?

There are three reasons why you need a sponsor.

Having a sponsor or accountability partner is biblical

Ecclesiastes 4:9–12 (GNB) tells us, "Two are better off than one, because together they can work more effectively. If one of them falls down, the other can help him up. But if someone is alone . . . , there is no one to help him. . . . Two men can resist an attack that would defeat one man alone."

Proverbs 27:17 tells us, "As iron sharpens iron, so one man sharpens another." The phrase "one another" is used in the New Testament over fifty times!

Having a sponsor or accountability partner is a key part of your recovery program

Do you know that your recovery program has four key elements to success? If your program includes each of these areas, you are well on your way to the solution, to wholeness.

The first key is maintaining your honest view of reality as you work each step. I have yet to see this program fail for someone who could be completely honest with himself or herself. I have, however, seen some give up on their recoveries because they could not step out of their denial into God's truth. Having someone help to keep you honest is a real plus in successfully working the steps.

The second key element is making your attendance at your recovery group meetings a priority in your schedule. This doesn't include taking the summer off or not going to a meeting because it's raining outside. Don't get me wrong, it's great to take a vacation, but after the two weeks are up, come back to your meetings. Remember, your hurts, hang-ups, and habits don't take vacations. You need to make Friday nights here at Celebrate Recovery and other meeting nights that you attend, a priority. A sponsor can encourage you to attend your meetings.

The third element is maintaining your spiritual program with Jesus Christ through prayer, meditation, and study of His Word. We are going to focus more on this in Principle 7, but you don't have to wait until you get there to develop your relationship with Christ. Your sponsor can pray for you and help to keep you centered on God's Word.

The last key element to a successful program is getting involved in service. Once you have completed Principle 8, you will be able to serve as a sponsor. Until that time, however, there are plenty of other service opportunities to get you started.

You know, service is nothing but love in work clothes, and there are plenty of opportunities to "suit up" for at Celebrate Recovery. We need help with the Bar-B-Que, with Solid Rock Cafe, passing out bulletins, and much more. If you want to get involved, see me, give me a call, or speak to your small group leader. Your sponsor can also suggest ways for you to serve.

Without exception, everyone here needs a sponsor or an accountability partner.

Having a sponsor is the best guard against relapse

By providing feedback to keep you on track, a sponsor can see your old dysfunctional, self-defeating patterns beginning to surface and point them out to you quickly. He or she can confront you with truth and love without placing shame or guilt.

Ecclesiastes 7:5 (TLB) tells us that "It is better to be criticized by a wise man than to be praised by a fool!" The trouble with most of us is that we would rather be ruined by praise than saved by criticism.

What Are the Qualities of a Sponsor?

"Though good advice lies deep within a counselor's heart, the wise man will draw it out" (Proverbs 20:5 TLB).

When you are selecting a sponsor look for the following qualities:

1. Does his walk match his talk? Is he living the eight principles? I have known many people that have the 12-Step "lingo" down pat. They can quote the Big Book of AA and even give page number references. But their lifestyle doesn't match their talk. Be certain that the person that you choose as a sponsor is someone whose life example is worthy of imitation.

2. Does she have a growing relationship with Jesus Christ? Do you see the character of Christ developing in her?

3. Does he express the desire to help others on the road to recovery? There is a difference between helping others and trying to fix others. We all need to be careful to guard the sponsorship relationship from becoming unhealthy and codependent.

4. Does she show compassion, care, and hope but not pity? You don't need someone to feel sorry for you, but you do need someone to be sensitive to your pain. As Pastor Rick (Warren) says, "People don't care about how much you know until they know about how much you care!"

5. Is he a good listener? Do you sense that he honestly cares about what you have to say?

6. Is she strong enough to confront your denial or procrastination? Does she care enough about you and your recovery to challenge you?

7. Does he offer suggestions? Sometimes we need help in seeing options or alternatives that we are unable to find on our own. A good sponsor can take an objective view and offer suggestions. He should not give orders!

8. Can she share her own current struggles with others? Is she willing to open up and be vulnerable and transparent? I don't know about you, but I don't want a sponsor who says that he has worked the principles. I want a sponsor who is living and working the principles every day!

What Is the Role of a Sponsor?

Let me give you six things that your sponsor can do:

1. She can be there to discuss issues in detail that are too personal or would take too much time in a meeting. This is especially true with Principle 4. You don't share your complete inventory in a group setting.

"I'm the lowest form of life on the earth" is a phrase often repeated by those doing their inventory. Others deny, rationalize, and blame: "Okay, I admit I did such and such, but it's not as if I killed anybody"; "Sure, I did a, b, and c, but my spouse did d through z; compared to my spouse, I'm a saint"; "All right, I admit it, but I never would have done it if my boss wasn't such a jerk."

The sponsor can be there to share his or her own experiences and to offer strength and hope: "You think you feel like a bum! Let me tell you how I felt when I did my inventory!" The sponsor's role is to model Christ's grace, forgiveness, and to give a sense of perspective.

2. He is available in times of crisis or potential relapse. I have always told the newcomers that I have sponsored, "Call me before you take that first drink. You can still take it after we talk, if you decide to. But please call first!" Remember Ecclesiastes 4:12 (GNB): "Two men can resist an attack that would defeat one man alone."

3. She serves as a sounding board by providing an objective point of view. This is especially true in Principle 6. When you are dealing with the sensitive area of making amends and offering forgiveness, you need a good sounding board.

4. He is there to encourage you to work the principles at your own speed. It is not his job to work the principles for you! He can coach your progress, confront you when you're stuck, and slow you down when you're working too fast.

5. Most important, she attempts to model the lifestyle that results from working the eight principles. It's difficult to inspire others to accomplish what you haven't been willing to try yourself. A good sponsor lives the principles.

6. A sponsor can resign or be fired. Sponsorship is not a lifetime position.

How Do I Find a Sponsor?

The responsibility of finding a sponsor is yours, but let me give you a few final guidelines to help you in your search.

1. First and foremost: Your sponsor MUST be of the same sex as you. NO EXCEPTIONS. I don't think I need to expand this one.

2. Can you relate to this person's story? Does he or she meet the qualities of a good sponsor that we just covered?

3. Come to the Bar-B-Que and the Solid Rock Cafe. Invest some time in fellowship and get to know others in your group. That's the main reason we have these fellowship events.

4. If you ask someone to sponsor you, and that person says no, do not take it as a personal rejection. Remember that their own recovery has to come first. Besides, they may already be sponsoring other people. I know a lot of you have asked your small group leader to be your sponsor. They all sponsor others, and the responsibility of leadership is great. If they turn you down, it's not personal. Their plate is simply too full! If someone turns you down, ask someone else! You can even ask for a "temporary sponsor." Remember, sponsorship is not a lifetime commitment.

5. Most important, ask God to lead you to the sponsor of His choosing. He knows you and everyone in this room. He has someone in mind already for you. All you need to do is ask!

What Is an Accountability Partner?

While the sponsor acts as a sort of recovery "coach," an accountability partner or group is a recovery "team." You can get with one, two, or three other people and hold each other accountable for certain areas of your recovery or issues such as meeting attendance, journaling, and so forth. These partners may be at the same or at a different level of recovery as you are. The main goal of this relationship is to encourage one another.

You can start forming accountability groups in your small groups tonight. When you share, just ask if anyone is interested. Let God work and see what happens. I can guarantee this, though, nothing will happen if you don't ask.

Start looking for and building your support team tonight!

Let's close in prayer.

Dear God, thank You for this group of people who are here to break out of the hurts, habits, and hang-ups that have kept them bound. Thank You for the leaders You have provided. Thank You that You love us all, no matter where we are in our recoveries. Show me the person You have prepared to be my sponsor. Help us to establish an honest and loving relationship that honors You and helps both me and my sponsor grow stronger in You. In Jesus' name I pray, AMEN.

PRINCIPLE 4 TESTIMONY

Hi, I'm Dee. I was raised in the suburbs of Minneapolis. I had one brother who was older than I and a sister and twin brothers who were younger. I was very fortunate in growing up. I had piano, tap, acrobat, and ballet lessons, and I was a Girl Scout. We grew up in a nice two-story home that my dad built, and we owned both a boat and a summer cabin that my dad built.

My mom stayed home when we were small children, but when my brother and I were old enough to care for the younger kids, she went to work full time. I felt I had a lot of responsibilities and chores growing up. I never felt I could please my mom. Everything had to be done just right, or when she got home from work she'd become very angry. We were never given a chance to talk to her. She told us the way it was going to be and then walked away. I was told never to sass, not to be selfish, and she'd say, "If you can't do something right, then don't do it at all." I grew up being the good girl. I thought if I did everything right and said what she wanted to hear, then she wouldn't get angry.

My dad retired after twenty years in the navy. He was thirty-eight years old. He then became a liquor salesman and did very well at it. We moved from our home to another, stayed for two years, and moved again. By now I was a junior in high school. Our huge new home was located on a beautiful lake. We had a dock with two boats, and two new cars in the driveway. The material things were always plentiful. I enjoyed the small, country high school I transferred to and joined as many extra-curricular activities as I could. I took secretarial courses because Mom believed girls didn't need to go to college: they get married, raise a family, and get office jobs.

I still didn't feel close to my mom. When I asked her if I could do something with friends, she'd say, "Go ask your father," or she'd say, "I don't know why you're asking me. You're going to do what you want, anyway." I never felt any support or approval from her.

When I was eighteen and graduated from high school, I got a good secretarial job and was still living at home. I moved out once in anger, but the place I chose to move to was not a good choice, and after one week I moved back home.

One January evening I was out ice skating with a girlfriend, and when I got back home, I heard that my sister, Linda, who was now sixteen years old, had been in a car accident. My dad and brother soon came home from the hospital and said Linda would be okay, but the doctor kept her overnight for observation. Mom had stayed with her.

At 4:00 A.M. I heard voices in the front hallway. It was Mom and Dad with the pastor from our church. Linda had died. How could that be? That only happens to other families, doesn't it? Dad blamed himself for Linda's death. He said if he'd given her the bigger car to drive and the one with seat belts, she'd still be with us. We couldn't talk about Linda's death. We all dealt with our grieving alone.

A year and a half later, we moved to California. I had a good job, lived on my own, and was attending community college. I met Butch, and one year later we were married. Three months after our wedding, Butch was sent to Vietnam for ten months. I lived with his family for six of those months, but then got my own apartment. Living with either set of parents did not work.

In 1973 and 1974, our two sons were born. In 1976, we bought our first home in Mission Viejo. Our new neighborhood had many young families like ourselves, and shortly after we moved in, a pastor and his family moved in nearby. We went to their church, Butch and I were baptized, and the boys were dedicated. I joined the women's neighborhood Bible study, and Butch and I joined the evening couples' Bible study. I was so thankful for this because in dealing with my sons, I would hear the anger in me, just like my mom. I began reading Dr. James Dobson's books on how to parent. The last thing I wanted was to sound like Mom.

As the boys grew, we had them in soccer, basketball, Little League, Indian Guides, and Boy Scouts. I was team mom, PTSA Vice President, Cubmaster, and I made team banners. I found that if I stayed busy, I didn't have to feel. Butch was gone a lot, either working late or having a drink with the guys. We'd talk about his drinking, but it never seemed to change things. When I'd call my mom to talk, she'd invite me over, and after a few drinks, I was fine.

In 1985, after living in our home for nine years, we decided to buy a larger home. I got a job at the new high school that was opening in the fall. We had a speaker at the first meeting I went to there who talked about substance abuse on our campuses. He gave us a paper on the characteristics of an alcoholic. I know I turned many shades of red as I read that paper. It hit home. I thought an alcoholic was a skid row bum. I didn't know it could be someone in my family.

In the fall of 1985, we moved to our new home. I started my new job, and three months later, the boys and I moved out. I started attending another church and found a support group at that church for AA and Al-Anon.

Butch and I were separated only a week when he said he'd go to AA meetings. We did this for three months, he at AA, I at Al-Anon, but then we quit. I figured if he didn't drink anymore, our problems were solved. As I worked at my new job at the high school, however, low self-esteem started getting the best of me. I was working with people who had bachelor's or master's degrees, and I was feeling less than everyone. I found it very difficult to talk to an authority figure without crying, and I didn't know how to say no when asked if I could do something. I always smiled, looked happy, got along with everyone, and pushed hard to do it all and to do it well. Their approval of me was my self-worth.

In my evaluation with my supervisor that year, she was concerned about my crying and said that it wasn't normal. She suggested that I get professional help. I left thinking, "Oh, I'm not that bad." I read a book that summer on self-image, and in the fall when we were back at school, I told her I was fine.

I started carpooling to meetings with a lady whom I had just started working with. We would talk and listen to a Christian psychologist on the radio, and I started hearing some things that I related to.

In October, 1992, I started seeing a Christian counselor whom she had recommended. It was here that I learned about codependency. Besides my weekly meeting with her, I went to codependency workshops and read a book on codependency three times! I was so glad to finally understand myself. My counselor suggested that I join a support group for codependent women and recommended Friday night Celebrate Recovery at Saddleback Church.

On Christmas Eve in 1992, we went to our first service in the tent, and in January, 1993, I came to Celebrate Recovery. I sat in the back of the tent and watched all of the people greeting each other and singing happy songs. I was scared about what was going on with me, felt very alone, and was very angry that I had to do this.

After two months of seeing my counselor, Butch and I began seeing her husband, who was also an MFCC. At this time my mom was diagnosed with bone marrow cancer and was going through radiation and chemotherapy. She was not doing well.

In June, 1993, Ryan graduated from high school, and in August we packed up both boys for college up north. I moved them into their new little house off the college campus and then drove back to Southern California, but I didn't stay. I quit my job, packed all of my personal belongings, and left for Northern California to go to my brother's home. I left friends, my job that I enjoyed, and my recovery program. My marriage wasn't good, and my boys were both gone, so I didn't think I had anything left here. My boss called me up north and said, "Dee, I can't hold your job open for you like I wanted. We're going to have to find a permanent replacement for you." I said, "That's not necessary. I'm coming back." I realized that I had made a big mistake. Once back home, I stayed with my dear friends, who never gave advice, only support. The first Friday night I returned to Celebrate Recovery, I saw Butch there, and he said he'd try again.

Well, I went back to work, moved back home, and started something new at Celebrate Recovery. In September, they were having a writing workshop, a spiritual journal. It would take nine months to complete, going every Friday night and working the twelve steps in the workbook. This is when I realized that I had *many* of the ACA characteristics. As I worked my 12-Step program, I realized the anger and fears I had, plus the feelings I had been suppressing.

At Step 4, I was working through a lot of anger I had for my mom and the blame I put on her for my problems. There was a lot of hurt and pain during this moral inventory, but I knew that I had come too far to turn around, and I was determined to get better.

As I reached the end of my 12-Step program, I did feel better about myself. I was beginning to express my feelings, not very tactfully at first, but getting in touch with how I felt. I worked through my fears of authority figures. I can now tell them what I *want* and *need*. I understand my feelings of abandonment now, and it's so good to know I'm not responsible for everything and that it's okay to say no!

Our marriage was still not good, and in the fall of 1994, I filed for divorce. We had been married for twenty-three years. It wasn't what I wanted, but I couldn't hang in there any longer. In my program, I learned that I could only change me, no one else. I had had many years of trying to "fix," "rescue," and "enable," and I was finally getting it—I had to detach.

I was now closer to God and felt a peace that He was in control and He would take care of me. I knew from my program that I only had to take one day at a time. On evening walks I would take my Celebrate Recovery song sheet and sing the songs that made me feel good, and I'd stop to meditate in the park before going home. I'd pray for God's guidance and His will for my life. I felt God's presence, and I knew that I was going to be okay.

In November, the Sunday before Thanksgiving, I put a prayer card in the offering basket and asked the prayer team to please pray for my husband. I felt he was on self-destruct. Three days later, Butch came back to his program.

It is now a year and a half later. In two weeks, we will celebrate our twenty-fifth wedding anniversary, and I believe it's only because of God and His will for our lives. If we had gone on our own wills, we would not be here—together—today.

My spiritual growth came slowly at the beginning. I struggled with "letting go and letting God." I wanted to fix all the defects in my life and in everyone else's, too. My progress is a product of God's help and a Christ-centered recovery program. I've learned that God's guidance is always available. All I need to do is listen, receive, and act without fear.

Psalm 27:1 says "The LORD is my light and my salvation—whom shall I fear? The LORD is the stronghold of my life—of whom shall I be afraid?"

Thanks for letting me share.

Inventory

Principle 4: Openly examine and confess my faults to myself, to God, and to someone I trust.

Happy are the pure in heart.

Step 4: We made a searching and fearless moral inventory of ourselves.

Let us examine our ways and test them, and let us return to the LORD.
Lamentations 3:40

Introduction

Tonight we are going to look at how to start your inventory, so get ready to write. Yes, that's right. Your inventory needs to be on paper. Writing (or typing) will help you organize your thoughts and focus on recalling events that you may have repressed. Remember you are not going through this alone. You are developing your support team to guide you; but even more importantly you are growing in your relationship with Jesus Christ!

Inventory

Ephesians 4:31 tells us to "Get rid of all bitterness, rage, and anger, brawling and slander, along with every form of malice."

The five-column inventory sheets in Participant's Guide 2 were developed to help you with this task. Let's take a look at each of the columns.

Column 1: "The Person"

In this column, you list the person or object you resent or fear. Go as far back as you can. Remember that resentment is mostly unexpressed anger and fear.

The good news is that as you work completely through Principle 4, you will see that your resentments fade as the light of your faith in Jesus Christ is allowed to shine on them!

Remember to list *all* the people and things that you are holding resentment against.

Column 2: "The Cause"

It has been said that "hurt people hurt people." In this column you are going to list the specific actions that someone did to hurt you. What did the person do to cause you resentment and/or fear? An example would be the alcoholic father that was emotionally unavailable for you as you were growing up. Another example would be the parent who attempted to control and dominate your life. This reflective look can be very painful, but that's why having a sponsor and an accountability team is essential. These people will be there to walk with you through the pain. Of course, Jesus will be with you too. God promises in Isaiah 41:10: "Fear not, for I am with you. Do not be dismayed. I am your God. I will strengthen you; I will help you; I will uphold you with my victorious right hand."

Column 3: "The Effect"

In this column write down how that specific hurtful action affected your life both in the past and in the present.

Column 4: "The Damage"

Which of your basic instincts were injured?

Social—Have you suffered from broken relationships, slander, or gossip?

Security—Has your physical safety been threatened? Have you faced financial loss?

Sexual—Have you been a victim in abusive relationships? Has intimacy or trust been damaged or broken?

No matter how you have been hurt, no matter how lost you may feel, God wants to comfort you and restore you. Remember Ezekiel 34:16 (GNB): "I will look for those that are lost, I will bring back those that wander off, bandage those that are hurt, and heal those that are sick."

Column 5: "My Part"

Lamentations 3:40 states: "Let us examine our ways and test them, and let us return to the LORD." It doesn't say, let us examine *their* ways. You did that already in the first four columns. Now you need to honestly determine the part of the resentment (or any other sin or injury) that *you* are responsible for. Ask God to show you *your* part in a broken or damaged marriage or relationship, a distant child or parent, or maybe a job lost. (You will use Column 5 later in Principle 6 when you work on becoming willing to make your amends.)

Psalm 139:23 (GNB) tells us: "Examine me, O God and know my mind; test me, and discover if there is any evil in me and guide me in the ever-lasting way."

Please note: If you have been in an abusive relationship, especially as a small child, you can find great freedom in this part of the inventory. You see that you had **NO** part, **NO** responsibility for the cause of the resentment. By simply writing the words **"NONE"** or **"NOT GUILTY"** in Column 5, you can begin to be free from the misplaced shame and guilt you have carried with you.

Celebrate Recovery has rewritten Step 4 for those that have been sexually or physically abused:

Made a searching and fearless moral inventory of ourselves, realizing all wrongs can be forgiven. Renounce the lie that the abuse was our fault.

Wrap-up

There are five tools to help you prepare your inventory:

1. Memorize Isaiah 1:18 (TLB): "Come, let's talk this over!" says the Lord; "no matter how deep the stain of your sins, I can take it out and make you as clean as freshly fallen snow. Even if you are stained as red as crimson, I can make you white as wool!"

2. Read the "balancing the scale verses" on page 27 of Participant's Guide 2!

3. Keep your inventory balanced. List both the good and the bad!

4. Continue to develop your support team.

5. Pray continuously.

Don't wait to start your inventory. Don't let any obstacle stand in your way. If you don't have a sponsor yet, talk to someone tonight! If you need a participant's guide, pick one up at the information table. Set a time and place and get busy! You *can* do it!

Spiritual Inventory Part 1

Principle 4: Openly examine and confess my faults to myself, to God, and to someone I trust.

Happy are the pure in heart.

Step 4: We made a searching and fearless moral inventory of ourselves.

Let us examine our ways and test them, and let us return to the LORD.
Lamentations 3:40

Introduction

Tonight we begin the first of two lessons in which we will look at our spiritual inventory, using the "Spiritual Evaluation" Pastor Rick Warren developed for this step.[1]

Principle 4 begins the process of coming clean, where you openly examine and confess your faults to yourself, to God, and to another person you trust.

[1]The eight areas of the spiritual inventory were written by Pastor Rick Warren. With his permission, I have added my teaching notes and comments.

Most of us don't like to look within ourselves for the same reason we don't like to open a letter that we know has bad news. But remember what we talked about in Lesson 9: You need to keep your evaluation, your inventory, balanced. It needs to include both the good and the bad within you. Let's look at what a spiritual inventory, or evaluation, is all about!

God's Word tells us, "Search me, O God, and know my heart; test my thoughts. Point out anything you find in me that makes you sad, and lead me along the path of everlasting life" (Psalm 139:23–24 TLB).

Do you know everyone has three different "characters"?

1. The character we exhibit.

2. The character we *think* we have.

3. The character we *truly* have.

No doubt each one has good qualities and bad. Tonight we are going to look at some of the bad, some of our character shortcomings and sins that can block us from receiving all the joy that God has intended. We will work on four areas of our character tonight and four more at our next session. This exercise will help you get started on your inventory as you search your heart!

Relationships with Others

In Matthew 6:12–14 (TLB) Jesus tells us to pray, "Forgive us our sins, just as we have forgiven those who have sinned against us. Don't bring us into temptation, but deliver us from the Evil One." Ask yourself the following questions regarding your relationships with others:

1. Who has hurt you?

2. Against whom have you been holding a grudge?

It doesn't take a doctor to tell you that it is better to remove a grudge than to nurse it. No matter how long you nurse a grudge, it won't get better. Writing the grudge down on your inventory is the first step in getting rid of it.

3. Against whom are you still seeking revenge?

Did you know that seeking revenge is like biting a dog just because the dog bit you? It really doesn't help you or the dog!

4. Are you jealous of someone?

In Songs of Songs 8:6 jealousy is said to be as unyielding as the grave. It burns like blazing fire!

5. Who have you been critical of or gossiped about?

It isn't that difficult to make a mountain out of a molehill. Just add a little dirt on it. That's what gossip is—just a little dirt!

I find it amazing that a tongue four inches long can destroy a man six feet tall. That's why James 1:26 tells us to "keep a tight rein on [our] tongue[s]."

6. Have you tried to justify your bad attitude by saying it is "their fault"?

I have found that when I'm searching for someone to blame, it's better for me to look in the mirror rather than through binoculars. Hosea 4:4 (NLT) tells us, "Don't point your finger at someone else and try to pass the blame."

The people that you name in this area will go in column 1 of your Celebrate Recovery Inventory (see Participant's Guide 2).

Next, let's look at what's important to you.

Priorities in Your Life

We do what is important to us. Others see our priorities by our actions, not our words. Personally, I'd rather see a sermon than hear one any day.

What are the priorities in your life?

Matthew 6:33 (TLB) tells us what will happen if we make God our number-one priority: "He will give ... to you if you give him first place in your life and live as he wants you to."

1. After making the decision to turn your life and your will over to God, in what areas of your life are you still not putting God first?

What closet are you not letting Him enter and clean out?

2.What, in your past, is interfering with your doing God's will?

Your ambition? Is it driven by serving God or is it driven by envy?

Your pleasures? If your pleasure has been found in the world, Proverbs 21:17 warns, "He who loves pleasure will become poor." Is your pleasure now found in Jesus Christ? Psalm 16:11 (NCV) tells us, "You will teach me how to live a holy life. Being with you will fill me with joy; at your right hand I will find pleasure forever."

3. What have been your priorities in your job? Friendships? Personal goals?

Were they just self-centered, self-serving? Selfishness turns life into a burden. Unselfishness turns burdens into life.

4. Who did your priorities affect?

You know, you will never get so rich that you can afford to lose a true friend.

5. What was good about your priorities?

6. What was wrong about them?

The next area of our spiritual inventory is to examine our attitudes.

Your Attitude

Ephesians 4:31 (GNB) says, "Get rid of all bitterness, passion, and anger. No more shouting or insults. No more hateful feelings of any sort."

1. Do you always try to have an "attitude of gratitude" or do you find yourself always complaining about your circumstances?

When you feel dog tired at night, do you ever think that it might be because you growled all day?

2. In what areas of your life are you ungrateful?

If we can't be grateful for the bad things in our lives that we have received, we can at least be thankful for what we have escaped.

And the one thing we can all be grateful for is found in 1 Corinthians 15:57: "But thanks be to God! He gives us the victory through our Lord Jesus Christ."

3. Have you gotten angry and easily blown up at people?

4. Have you been sarcastic?

Do you know that sarcasm can be a form of verbal abuse?

5. What in your past is still causing you fear or anxiety?

As we have said before, your fear imprisons you; your faith liberates you. Fear paralyzes; faith empowers! Fear disheartens; faith encourages! Fear sickens; faith heals! Faith in Jesus Christ will allow you to face your past fears, and with faith you can be free of fear's chains. First John 4:18 says, "There is no fear in love. But perfect love drives out fear, because fear has to do with punishment. The one who fears is not made perfect in love."

The last area we are going to talk about tonight is your integrity.

Your Integrity

Colossians 3:9 (NCV) tells us, "Do not lie to each other. You have left your old sinful life and the things you did before."

1. In what past dealing were you dishonest?

An honest man alters his ideas to fit the truth. A dishonest man alters the truth to fit his ideas.

2. Have you stolen things?

I told you that your inventory wasn't going to be easy.

3. Have you exaggerated yourself to make yourself look better?

Do you know, there are no degrees of "honest": Either you are or you aren't!

4. In what areas of your past have you used false humility?

Did you know that humility is never gained by seeking it? To think we have it is sure proof that we don't.

5. Have you pretended to live one way in front of your Christian friends and another way at home or at work?

Are you a "Sunday Christian" or a seven-day, full-time follower of Jesus Christ? Do you try to practice the eight principles seven days a week or just here at Celebrate Recovery on Friday nights?

Wrap-up

Well, that's enough to work on for one week, but next week we'll dig in again and look at Part 2 of our spiritual inventory. We'll explore our old ways of thinking—our minds, the ways we have treated or mistreated God's temple—our bodies, how we did or didn't walk by faith in the past, our important past relations with our family and church.

As you start to work on your spiritual inventory, remember two things. First, in Isaiah 1:18 (TLB) God says, "No matter how deep the stain of your sins, I can take it out and make you as clean as freshly fallen snow." Second—I can't say it enough—Keep your inventory balanced. List the positive new relationships that you have, the areas of your life that you have been able to turn over to God, how your attitude has improved since you have been in recovery, the ways you have been able to step out of your denial into God's truth.

Let's close in prayer.

Father God, thank You for each person here tonight. Thank You for giving them the courage to begin this difficult step of making an inventory. Give them the desire and strength they need to proceed. Encourage them and light their way with Your truth. In the strong name of Jesus I pray, AMEN.

Lesson 11

Spiritual Inventory Part 2

Principle 4: Openly examine and confess my faults to myself, to God, and to someone I trust.

Happy are the pure in heart.

Step 4: We made a searching and fearless moral inventory of ourselves.

Let us examine our ways and test them, and let us return to the LORD.
Lamentations 3:40

Introduction

Tonight we are looking at the second part of our spiritual inventory, where we pray, "Search me, O God, and know my heart; test my thoughts. Point out anything you find in me that makes you sad, and lead me along the path of everlasting life" (Psalm 139:23–24 TLB).

Last week, we discussed in Part 1 of our spiritual inventories four areas of our lives. We asked ourselves some hard questions.

We looked at our relationships to others, our priorities, our attitudes, and our integrity. We talked about how our past actions in each of these areas had a negative or a positive effect on our lives and the lives of others.

Tonight, we are going to finish our spiritual inventory. We will look for some of our additional shortcomings or sins that can prevent God from working effectively in our lives and our recoveries.

Evaluating each area will help you complete your inventory.

Your Mind

Did you know that the most difficult thing to open is a closed mind?

Romans 12:2 gives us clear direction regarding our minds: "Do not conform any longer to the pattern of this world, but be transformed by the renewing of your mind. Then you will be able to test and approve what God's will is—his good, pleasing and perfect will."

Some questions to ask yourself in this area:

1. How have you guarded your mind in the past? What did you deny?

Once again you need to see and examine how your coping skills—your denial—may have protected you from pain and hurt in the past. It may have done so, however, by preventing you from living in and dealing with reality.

Do you know that two thoughts cannot occupy your mind at the same time? It is your choice as to whether your thoughts will be constructive or destructive, positive or negative.

2. Have you filled your mind with hurtful and unhealthy movies, television programs, magazines, or books?

Your ears and your eyes are doors and windows to your soul. So, remember "garbage in, garbage out."

Straight living cannot come out of crooked thinking. It just is not going to happen.

Remember Proverbs 15:14 (NLT): "A wise person is hungry for truth, while a fool feeds on trash."

3. Have you failed to concentrate on the positive truths of the Bible?

I believe that three of the greatest sins today are indifference to, neglect of, and disrespect for the Word of God. Have you set aside a daily quiet time to get into God's instruction manual for your life?

Next, let's look at how we have treated our bodies. Did you know that with proper care the human body will last a lifetime?

Your Body

"Haven't you yet learned that your body is the home of the Holy Spirit God gave you, and that he lives within you? Your own body does not belong to you. For God has bought you with a great price. So use every part of your body to give glory back to God, because he owns it" (1 Corinthians 6:19–20 TLB).

1. In what ways have you mistreated your body?

Have you abused alcohol, drugs, food, or sex? This was, and still is, a tough one for me. In the depth of my alcoholism my weight dropped down to 160 pounds (my normal weight is 220 pounds). I almost died. I kept getting my suit pants taken in, and finally, the tailor explained to me that he couldn't take them in any more—the back pockets were touching. I asked God to help me get my strength and weight back. He truly blessed me. Boy, did He bless me! Now, it's time for moderation in my eating.

It is through our bodies or flesh that Satan works, but thank God that the believer's body is the temple of the Holy Spirit. God freely gives us the grace of His Spirit. He values us so much that He chose to place His Spirit within us. We need to have as much respect for ourselves as our Creator does for us.

2. What activities or habits caused harm to your physical health?

Remember, it was the God of creation who made you. Look at Psalm 139:13–14, 16: "For you created my inmost being; you knit me together in my mother's womb. I praise you because I am fearfully and wonderfully made; your works are wonderful, I know that full well. . . . Your eyes saw my unformed body. All the days ordained for me were written in your book before one of them came to be."

Many people say that they have the right to do whatever they want to their own bodies. Although they think that this is freedom, they really become enslaved to their own desires, which ultimately cause them great harm.

Your Family

In the Old Testament, Israel's leader, Joshua, made a bold statement regarding his household: "If you are unwilling to obey the Lord, then decide today whom you will obey. . . . But as for me and my family, we will serve the Lord" (Joshua 24:15 TLB).

1. Have you mistreated anyone in your family? How?

Perhaps you have physically or emotionally mistreated your family. Emotional abuse doesn't have to take the form of raging, yelling, or screaming. Tearing down a child's or spouse's self-esteem and being emotionally unavailable to them are both ways you may have harmed your loved ones.

God designed families to be our safety from life's storms. As much as it depends on you, you need to provide a haven for your family. If that isn't possible and you yourself don't feel safe there, let Celebrate Recovery be your family.

2. Against whom in your family do you have a resentment?

This can be a difficult area in which to admit your true feelings. It's easier to admit the resentments you have against a stranger or someone at work than someone in your own family. Denial can be a pretty thick fog to break through here. But you need to do it if you are going to successfully complete your inventory.

3. To whom do you owe amends?

You identify them now and work on becoming willing to deal with amends in Principle 6. All you are really looking for is your part in a damaged relationship.

4. What is the family secret that you have been denying?

What is the "pink elephant" in the middle of your family's living room that no one talks about? That's the family secret! Remember Jeremiah 6:14 (TLB): "You can't heal a wound by saying it's not there."

Your Church

One of the main reasons I started Celebrate Recovery was that I found most members of secular 12-Step groups knew the Lord's Prayer much better that they knew the Lord.

"Let us not neglect our church meetings, as some people do, but encourage and warn each other, especially now that the day of his coming back again is drawing near" (Hebrews 10:25 TLB).

1. Have you been faithful to your church in the past?

Your church is like a bank: the more you put into it, the more interest you gain in it.

2. Have you been critical instead of active?

If you don't like something in your church, get involved so you can help change it or at least understand it better. Turn your grumbling into service!

3. Have you discouraged your family's support of their church?

If you aren't ready to get involved in your church, that's your decision. But don't stop the rest of your family from experiencing the joys and support of a church family!

Wrap-up

We've made it all the way through the eight different areas to help you begin and complete your inventory.

Once again, listen to Isaiah 1:18. Memorize it! God says, "No matter how deep the stain of your sins, I can take it out and make you as clean as freshly fallen snow."

A couple of reminders as we close:

- Use the "Balancing the Scales" verses found in Participant's Guide 2.

- Keep your inventory balanced. List your strengths along with your weaknesses.

- Find an accountability partner or a sponsor. I cannot say this enough: The road to recovery is not a journey to be made alone!

God bless you as you courageously face and own your past. He *will* see you through!

Confess

Principle 4: Openly examine and confess my faults to myself, to God, and to someone I trust.

Happy are the pure in heart.

Step 5: We admitted to God, to ourselves, and to another human being the exact nature of our wrongs.

Therefore confess your sins to each other and pray for each other so that you may be healed.

James 5:16

Introduction

The following illustration is part of a message on Step 5, which, of course, corresponds to our Principle 4. I heard it at Willow Creek Church, and it is undoubtedly the best illustration that I have found to represent this principle.

Does the name Jessica McClure trip any memory bells in your mind? She was the eighteen-month-old girl from Midland, Texas, who fell in a deep abandoned well-pipe a few years ago. About four hundred people took part in her fifty-eight-hour rescue attempt, which was spurred on by her cries of anguish that could be clearly heard at ground level through the pipe.

Now, I found it fascinating that, at one point, a critical decision was made. The rescuers decided that the rescue would have two phases: Phase one was to simply get somebody down there, next to her, as soon as possible; phase two was actually extracting her from the well.

Phase one was driven by the knowledge that people tend to do and think strange things when they are trapped alone in a dark scary place for long periods of time. They get disorientated and their fears get blown out of proportion. Their minds play tricks on them. Sometimes they start doing self-destructive things. Sometimes they just give up! So the rescue experts decided that they needed to get a person down there to be with her as soon as possible. Then they would turn their attention on how they were going to get her out of the well. The plan worked, and eventually Jessica was rescued.

Now, how does the rescue of Jessica McClure relate to Step 5?

When people like us get serious about recovery, about spiritual growth, when we go on the 12-Step spiritual adventure, when we take that first step, we admit that we have some problems that make our lives unmanageable. When we turn to God and say, "God, I need help with those problems," then we might feel as though we are free falling. In a sense we are. We are out of control in a way. We can no longer live the way we are so used to living. The old ways just don't work anymore.

To complicate matters, on the way down, you find that the problem that you admitted in Step 1 is really being driven by a whole collection of character defects, which have been growing five feet under the surface of your life. And you have to identify those defects. You have to inventory them, as we have talked about for the last two months. You have to list them, admit them, and own them. You need to take responsibility for your pride, anger, envy, lust, greed, gluttony, and sloth. You know, "the big seven."

So, during the last couple of months, if you worked Step 4 honestly and thoroughly, you might be feeling as if *you* are trapped at the bottom of a deep, dark well. If you stay there long enough you can become disoriented and wonder why you took this recovery journey to begin with. You might feel like you want to bail out at this point.

You might start making statements like these: "You know that I am a royally messed up man." "The truth about me is that I'm a royally messed up woman." "No one's collection of sins and character defects is as bad as mine." "If anyone ever found out the truth about me, they would never have anything to do with me for the rest of their life."

Some of you get to that point and you say, "Why don't I just bail out of this program? Why don't I just go back to projecting an image of adequacy to everybody and not deal with all this unsettling truth about myself?"

It's at this critical point in the process that we need to get another human being to come alongside of us in that well as soon as possible. You need to get someone next to you before you give up and get back into denial. In a way, the Fifth Step says that you can only grow so far alone; then you reach the point that continued growth and healing is going to require assistance from someone else.

We are right at that critical juncture tonight. We are at the point where we are being asked to come clean by telling another human being the truth about who we really are. But how?

Confess

The first step is to CONFESS my wrongs. Tonight's acrostic will show you just how to do that.

Confess your shortcomings, resentments, and sins

Obey God's direction

No more guilt

Face the truth

Ease the pain

Stop the blame

Start accepting God

The *C* in confess is CONFESS your shortcomings, resentments, and sins. God wants us to *come clean* and admit that wrong is wrong, that we're "guilty as charged." We need to "own up" to the sins we discovered in our inventory.

For the person who confesses, shame is over and realities have begun. Proverbs 28:13 tells us, "He who conceals his sins does not prosper, but whoever confesses and renounces them finds mercy." Confession is necessary for fellowship. Our sins have built a barrier between us and God.

The *O* in confess stands for OBEY God's direction.

Confession means that we agree with God regarding our sins. Confession restores our fellowship.

Principle 4 sums up how to obey God's direction in confessing our sins. First, we confessed [admitted] our faults to ourselves, to God, and to someone we trust. "'As surely as I am the living God, says the Lord, everyone will kneel before me, and everyone will confess that I am God.' Every one of us, then, will have to give an account of himself to God" (Romans 14:11–12 GNB).

Then we do what we are instructed to do in James 5:16: "Confess your sins to each other and pray for each other so that you may be healed."

The next letter is *N:* No more guilt.

This principle can restore our confidence, our relationships, and allow us to move on from our "rear-view mirror" way of living that kept us looking back and second-guessing ourselves and others.

In Romans 8:1 (GNB) we are assured that "There is no condemnation now for those who live in union with Christ Jesus." The verdict is in! "All have sinned; ... yet God declares us 'not guilty' ... if we trust in Jesus Christ, who freely takes away our sins" (Romans 3:23–24 TLB).

So that's the "C-O-N" of confess. The "con" is over! We have followed God's directions on how to confess our wrongs.

After we "fess" up, we will have four positive changes in our lives. The first is that we will be able to FACE the truth. It has been said that "man occasionally stumbles over the truth, but most of the time he will pick himself up and continue on." Recovery doesn't work like that. Recovery *requires* honesty! "Jesus ... said, 'I am the light of the world. Whoever follows me will never walk in darkness, but will have the light of life'" (John 8:12).

Have you ever noticed that a man who speaks the truth is always at ease? The next positive change that confession brings is to EASE the pain.

We are only as sick as our secrets! When we share our deepest secrets, we begin to divide the pain and the shame. A healthy self-worth develops that is no longer based on the world's standards, but based on the truth of Jesus Christ!

Pain is inevitable for all of us, but misery is optional. Psalm 32:3–5 (TLB) says, "There was a time when I wouldn't admit what a sinner I was. But my dishonesty made me miserable and filled my days with frustration. . . . My strength evaporated like water on a sunny day until I finally admitted all my sins to you and stopped trying to hide them. I said to myself, 'I will confess them to the Lord.' And you forgave me! All my guilt is gone."

The first *S* in confess reminds us that we can now STOP the blame.

It has been said that a man who can smile when things go wrong probably just thought of somebody he can blame it on. But the truth is, we cannot find peace and serenity if we continue to blame ourselves or others. Our secrets have isolated us from each other long enough! They have prevented intimacy in all of our important relationships.

Jesus tells us in Matthew 7:3 (PHILLIPS): "Why do you look at the speck of sawdust in your brother's eye and fail to see the plank in your own? How can you say to your brother, 'Let me get the speck out of your eye,' when there is a plank in your own? . . . Take the plank out of your own eye first, and then you can see clearly enough to remove your brother's speck of dust."

Finally, the last *S* shows us that it is time to START accepting God's forgiveness. Once we accept God's forgiveness we are able to look others in the eye. We see ourselves and our actions in a new light. We are ready to find the humility to exchange our shortcomings in Principle 5.

"For God was in Christ, restoring the world to himself, no longer counting men's sins against them but blotting them out" (2 Corinthians 5:19 TLB).

If you asked me to sum up the benefits of Principle 4 in one sentence it would be this: In confession we open our lives to the healing, reconciling, restoring, uplifting grace of Jesus Christ who loves us in spite of ourselves.

First John 1:9 (NCV) reminds us that "if we confess our sins, he will forgive our sins, because we can trust God to do what is right. He will cleanse us from all the wrongs we have done."

Wrap-up

Maybe you came tonight a little fearful of having to think about sharing your inventory. I hope you have been encouraged, and I trust you have been able to see the benefits of this task before you. Next time we will discuss the how-tos of finding a person with whom you can share your inventoy. Let's close in prayer.

Dear God, thank You for your promise that if we confess, You will hear us and cleanse us, easing our pain and guilt. Thank You that You always do what is right. In Jesus' name, AMEN.

Lesson 13

Admit

Principle 4: Openly examine and confess my faults to myself, to God, and to someone I trust.

Happy are the pure in heart.

Step 5: We admitted to God, to ourselves, and to another human being the exact nature of our wrongs.

Therefore confess your sins to each other and pray for each other so that you may be healed.

James 5:16

Introduction

This week we are going to focus on confessing (admitting) our sins, all the dark secrets of our past, to another person.

We have all heard that the wages of sin is death, but you may not have heard that the wages of sin are never frozen or that they are never subject to income taxes. One of the main reasons for that is because most of the wages of sin go unreported! And, by the way, if the wages of sin is death, shouldn't you quit before payday?

Why Admit My Wrongs?

All joking aside, this part of Principle 4 is often difficult for people. I am often asked, "Why do I have to admit my wrongs to another?"

Many of us have been keeping secrets almost all of our lives. Every day those secrets take a toll on us. The toll we pay is loss of self-respect and energy and bondage to old codependent habits. Admitting—out loud—those secrets strips them of their power. They lose much of their hold on us when they are spoken.

Still, we are afraid to reveal our secrets to another person, even someone we trust. We somehow feel like we have everything to lose and nothing to gain. I want you to hear the truth tonight. Do you know what we *really* have to lose by telling our secrets and sins to another?

1. We lose our sense of isolation. Somebody is going to come down into that well we talked about two weeks ago and be alongside us. Our sense of aloneness will begin to vanish.

2. We will begin to lose our unwillingness to forgive. When people accept and forgive us, we start to see that we can forgive others.

3. We will lose our inflated, false pride. As we see and accept who we are, we begin to gain true humility, which involves seeing ourselves as we really are and seeing God as He really is.

4. We will lose our sense of denial. Being truthful with another person will tear away our denial. We begin to feel clean and honest.

Now that you know what you have to *lose* when you admit your wrongs to another, let me tell you three benefits you will *gain*.

1. We gain healing that the Bible promises. Look at James 5:16 again: "Confess your sins to each other and pray for each other so that you may be healed." The key word here is *healed*. The verse doesn't say, "confess your sins to one another and you will be forgiven." God *forgave* you when you confessed your sins to *Him*. Now He says you will begin the healing process when you confess your sins to *another*.

2. We gain freedom. Our secrets have been kept in chains—bound, frozen, unable to move forward in any of our relationships with God and others. Admitting our sins *snaps* the chains so God's healing power can start.

"They cried to the Lord in their troubles, and he rescued them! He led them from the darkness and the shadow of death and snapped their chains" (Psalm 107:13–14 TLB).

Unconfessed sin, however, will fester. In Psalm 32:3–4 (GNB) David tells us what happened to him when he tried to hide his sins: "When I did not confess my sins, I was worn out from crying all day long.... My strength was completely drained." Remember, "Openness is to wholeness as secrets are to sickness." My grandpa used to say, "If you want to clear the stream, you need to get the hog out of the spring." Admit and turn from your sins. Remember that the only sin God can't forgive is the one that is not confessed.

3. We gain support. When you share your inventory with another person, you get support! The person can keep you focused and provide feedback. When your old friend "denial" surfaces and you hear Satan's list of excuses— "It's really not that bad"; "They deserved it"; "It really wasn't my fault"—your support person can be there to challenge you with the truth. But most of all, you need another person simply to listen to you and hear what you have to say.

How Do I Choose Someone?

Unlike little Jessica, the little girl trapped in the well, whom we talked about in Lesson 12, you can choose the person to come down into your well with you, so choose carefully! You don't want someone to say, "You did what?" or "You shouldn't have done that." You don't need a judge and jury. We already talked about the verdict. Remember Romans 3:23–24 (TLB): "All have sinned; ... yet now God declares us 'not guilty' ... if we trust in Jesus Christ, who ... freely takes away our sins" and 1 John 1:9: "If we confess our sins, he is faithful and just and he will forgive our sins and purify us from all unrighteousness"?

You just need someone to listen. I find that it works best to choose someone who is a growing Christian and is familiar with the eight principles or the 12 Steps.

1. Choose someone of the same sex as you whom you trust and respect. Enough said!

2. Ask the person if he or she has completed Principle 4 or Steps 4 and 5. The process should go more smoothly if the person is familiar with what you are doing. He or she will also have a sense of empathy, and if the person can share personal experiences, you will have a healthy exchange.

3. Set an appointment with the person, a time without interruptions! Get away from the telephones, kids, all interruptions for at least two hours. I have heard of some inventories that have taken eight hours to share. That's perhaps a little dramatic.

Guidelines for Your Meeting

1. Start with prayer. Ask for courage, humility, and honesty. Here is a sample prayer for you to consider:

> *God, I ask that You fill me with Your peace and strength during my sharing of my inventory. I know that You have forgiven me for my past wrongs, my sins. Thank You for sending Your Son to pay the price for me, so my sins can be forgiven. During this meeting help me be humble and completely honest. Thank You for providing me with this program and* _____ *(the name of the person with whom you are sharing your inventory). Thank You for allowing the chains of my past to be snapped. In my Savior's name I pray, AMEN.*

2. Read the Principle 4 verses found on page 22 in Participant's Guide 3, *Getting Right with God, Yourself, and Others.*

3. Keep your sharing balanced—weaknesses and strengths!

4. End in prayer. Thank God for the tools He has given to you and for the complete forgiveness found in Christ!

PRINCIPLE 4 TESTIMONY

My name is John, a believer and a recovering alcoholic who has identified Jesus Christ as my Higher Power. I will not bore you with the details of my twenty-nine-and-a-half years of compulsive and uncontrollable drinking; the damage can be summarized as follows:

0 self-worth
1 broken and abandoned family
2 divorces
3 502s or DUIs
4 trips to jail
5 years without filing income tax
6 emergency trips to the hospital
countless attempts to *control* my drinking

blood pressure of 190/165!
265 pounds of cheap vodka and Valium

Worse than all this, I was spiritually and morally bankrupt and had lost the "game of life." On January 7, 1976, after a very drunken holiday season and an emotional encounter with my mother and other members of my family, my "moment of clarity" revealed that I could no longer go on, and I called AA.

Unknown to me, the great spiritual journey had begun. I did not know, nor could I understand the words of Ephesians 2:10: "We are God's workmanship, created in Christ Jesus to do good works, which God prepared in advance for us to do."

For the next fifteen years, I prospered financially and physically with my secular AA program. When I did my Fourth Step, that is "Made a searching and fearless moral inventory of myself," I just started writing and writing and writing. What came out of three notebooks full was the following:

1. Expectations were catastrophic to me, a real fear of failure and not meeting what I perceived to be the expectations of others was with me from earliest childhood. My dad died when I was three. He was a prominent physician, just getting started during the Great Depression, the pride of the whole family, and from the earliest days I can remember the family talk: "Look at John's hands, won't he make a wonderful surgeon, just like his father." Or, "John has been pre-admitted to medical school at his father's alma mater; he'll be just like his father."

All this responsibility placed on me by others turned into *guilt* and *resentment*, which I buried and carried with me for years.

2. Loneliness or fear of rejection was a companion of my fear of not meeting the expectations of others; although I wanted validation, I felt alone and isolated because I was an only child. Even though I was always in a crowd or part of group, my Fourth Step made me aware that I was alone. I had pushed away the people I was seeking approval from. One by one, I had lost those that were important to me and I was a master at putting the blame on others.

3. I can conclude my Fourth Step comments by mentioning that woven in through all of this was a fear of losing control. But with enough alcohol, a "charming personality," and a certain amount of hard work, you would never know that all this was going on inside me. Talk about beating myself up! I was committing suicide on the installment plan, with twenty-nine-and-a-half years of daily drinking.

With a Fourth Step, plus much more that filled those notebooks, my writing revealed that I was able to see things as they really were, to accept the reality of my life, and to accept the responsibility (ownership) for all the damage I had done.

Soon, I took the Fifth Step and admitted the exact nature of my wrongs to myself and to another human being. Now, as you all know, the Fifth Step says that we admit the exact nature of our wrongs to *God*, to ourselves, and to another human being. I did not have, nor did I want, God in my life at that time, so I left God out of the loop. I never was able to forgive myself or accept God's forgiveness for my sins against those I hurt. As I said, I had been sober fifteen years and working a good 12-Step program, involved with H & I and other twelfth-step work, but there was an emptiness that tormented me. I would cry out, "Is this all there is to sobriety? There must be more to life than this!" You see, there is one thing I haven't told you—I belonged to the CIA!

Yes, the CIA: Catholic, Irish, and Alcoholic. I thought the Catholic religion was rigid and unforgiving and that God had abandoned me. This was not true. All Irish, as you know, are stubborn, opinionated, and basically "full of blarney." This could possibly be true. As a recovering alcoholic, I was still in denial and I denied that I needed God in my life. I was wrong, of course. Some big unknown piece was missing and I was miserable. I could no longer deny that I needed God in my life, I had to find a church.

And now we get to the miracle!

About a week after I had decided to find a church, I found a flyer on my doorstep announcing the 1991 Easter service at Saddleback. I have since learned that this is the only year that Saddleback did a mailing to the Capistrano Valley area about twenty-five miles away. Is this a coincidence? I think not!

At Easter service 1991, I heard this message:

Trust God—the past is forgiven.
Trust God—the present is manageable.
Trust God—the future is secure.

I broke down and cried throughout the sermon. I felt the presence of the Holy Sprit welcoming me home, and my loneliness and fear were gone.

I ran home and told my wife what had happened, and she could see the joy, peace, and presence of God's Holy Spirit. The rest is history.

I took all the classes at Saddleback for membership, maturity, and ministry. I was baptized in September of 1991. In my ministry interview, Pastor Steve packed me off to Pastor John Baker in Celebrate Recovery, and I began setting up the chairs on Friday night and helping in any other way that I could.

I was asked to be a small group leader for a group of chemically dependent men, all new to recovery. Our first ninety-day program is now in its third year, and I have had the privilege of leading dozens of men through the first three principles in the Celebrate Recovery participant's guides.

My daily life is now greatly involved with the Christian recovering brothers, working a Christ-centered 12-Step program, still helping out wherever I can, and seeing, in so many ways, the healing, restored relationships, and miracles that only a relationship with Jesus Christ can provide.

In working my own Christ-centered 12-Step program, I was finally able to complete Step 5, and accept God's forgiveness and love, through Christ's work on the cross. My sins were forgiven, my guilt and fears were removed. I can clearly see God's plan and purpose for my life.

In closing, let me reference one verse that I can now truly understand and accept, 2 Corinthians 5:17 (TLB): "When someone becomes a Christian he becomes a brand new person inside. He is not the same any more. A new life has begun!"

Thank you for letting me share a small miracle with you.

Principle 5

Voluntarily submit to every change God wants to make in my life and humbly ask Him to remove my character defects.

"Happy are those whose greatest desire is to do what God requires."

Ready

Principle 5: Voluntarily submit to every change God wants to make in my life and humbly ask Him to remove my character defects.

Happy are those whose greatest desire is to do what God requires.

Step 6: We were entirely ready to have God remove all these defects of character.

Humble yourselves before the Lord, and he will lift you up.

James 4:10

Introduction

Congratulations! If you are ready for Principle 5, you have already taken some major steps on the road to recovery. You admitted you had a problem and were powerless over it; you came to believe that God could and would help you; you sought Him and turned your life and your will over to His care and direction; you wrote a spiritual inventory and shared that with God and another person. You've been busy! That's a lot of work—hard work!

Maybe you're thinking that it's about time to take a breather and relax for a while. Think again!

In AA material, Step 6 (Principle 5) has been referred to as the step "that separates the men from the boys"! So tonight we are going to answer the question, "What does it mean to be entirely READY?"

Ready

One of the reasons that Principle 5 "separates the men from the boys"—or the women from the girls, for that matter—is because it states that we are ready to "voluntarily submit to every change God wants to make in my life."

Most of us, if not all of us, would be very willing to have *certain* character defects go away. The sooner the better! But let's face it, some defects are hard to give up.

I'm an alcoholic, but there came a time in my life, a moment of clarity, when I knew I had hit bottom and was ready to stop drinking. But was I ready to stop lying? Stop being greedy? Ready to let go of resentments? I had been doing these things for a long time. Like weeds in a garden, they had developed roots!

We've formed our defects of character, our hang-ups, our habits over periods of ten, twenty, or thirty years. In this principle you and God—together—are going after these defects. *All* of them!

Tonight's acrostic will show you how to get READY to allow Him to do that.

Release control

Easy does it

Accept the change

Do replace your character defects

Yield to the growth

The first letter tonight stands for RELEASE control. That reminds me of a story I heard.

A man bumped into an old friend in a bar. He said, "I thought you gave up drinking. What's the matter, no self-control?" The friend replied, "Sure I've got plenty of self-control. I'm just too strong-willed to use it!"

God is very courteous and patient. In Principle 3, He didn't impose His will on you. He waited for you to invite Him in!

Now in Principle 5, you need to be "entirely ready," willing to let God into every area of your life. He won't come in and clean up an area unless you are willing to ask Him in.

It has been said that "willingness is the key that goes into the lock and opens the door that allows God to begin to remove your character defects." I love the way the psalmist invites God to work in his life: "Help me to do your will, for you are my God. Lead me in good paths, for your Spirit is good" (Psalm 143:10 TLB).

Simply put, the *R*—release control—is "Let go; let God!"

The *E* in ready stands for EASY does it. These principles and steps are not quick fixes! You need to allow time for God to work in your life.

This principle goes further than just helping you stop doing wrong. Remember, the sin is the *symptom* of the character defect.

Let me explain. The sin is like a weed in a garden: It will keep reappearing unless it is pulled out by the roots. And the roots are the actual defects of character that *cause* the particular sin. In my case, the major sin in my life was abusing alcohol. That was the act, the sin. The defect of character was my lack of any positive self-image. So, when I worked Principle 5, I went after the defect—my lack of a positive self-image—that caused me to sin by abusing alcohol.

That takes time, but God will do it. He promised! "Commit everything you do to the Lord. Trust him to help you do it and he will" (Psalm 37:5 TLB).

The next letter is *A*: ACCEPT the change.

Seeing the need for change and allowing the change to occur are two different things, and the space between recognition and willingness can be filled with fear. Besides that, fear can trigger our old dependency on self-control. But this principle will not work if we are still trapped by our self-will. We need to be ready to accept God's help throughout the transition. The Bible makes this very clear in 1 Peter 1:13–14 (GNB): "So then, have your minds ready for action. Keep alert and set your hope completely on the blessing which will be given you when Jesus Christ is revealed. Be obedient to God, and do not allow your lives to be shaped by those desires you had when you were still ignorant."

As I said, all the steps you have taken on the road to recovery have helped you build the foundation for the "ultimate surrender" that is found in Principle 5.

James 4:10 says, "Humble yourselves before the Lord, and he will lift you up." All we need is the willingness to let God lead on us on our road to recovery.

Let's move on to the *D* in ready, which is extremely important: DO replace your character defects.

You spent a lot of time with your old hang-ups, compulsions, obsessions, and habits. When God removes one, you need to replace it with something positive, such as recovery meetings, church activities, twelfth-step service, and volunteering! If you don't, you open yourself for a negative character defect to return.

Listen to Matthew 12:43–45 (GNB): "When an evil spirit goes out of a person, it travels over dry country looking for a place to rest. If it can't find one, it says to itself, 'I will go back to my house.' So it goes back and finds the house empty, . . . then it goes out and brings along seven other spirits even worse than itself, and they come to live there."

I said that one of my major defects of character was a negative self-image, a nonexistent self-esteem, to be more exact. I wasted a lot of time in bars, attempting to drown it. When I started working the 12 Steps, I found I had lots of time on my hands. I tried to fill it by doing positive things that would build my self-esteem, rather than tear it down.

In addition to working my program and attending meeting after meeting, I fellowshiped and worked with "healthy" people. I volunteered. As the months passed, I got more involved at church, too. That's when God called me to start to build Celebrate Recovery. I started going to seminary.

You don't have to start a ministry, but you do have to replace your negative character defect with something positive. There are many, many opportunities to serve and get involved in at church.

The last letter in ready is the *Y:* YIELD to the growth.

At first, your old self-doubts and low self-image may tell you that you are not worthy of the growth and progress you are making in the program. Don't listen! Yield to the growth. It is the Holy Spirit's work within you.

"The person who has been born into God's family does not make a practice of sinning, because now God's life is in him; so he can't keep on sinning, for this new life has been born into him and controls him—he has been *born again*" (1 John 3:9 TLB).

Wrap-up

The question is, "Are you entirely ready to voluntarily submit to any and all changes God wants to make in your life?"

If you are, then read the Principle 5a verses found in Participant's Guide 3 on page 28, and pray the following prayer:

> *Dear God, thank You for taking me this far in my recovery journey. Now I pray for Your help in making me be entirely ready to change all my shortcomings. Give me the strength to deal with all of my character defects that I have turned over to You. Allow me to accept all the changes that You want to make in me. Help me be the person that You want me to be. In Your Son's name I pray, AMEN.*

Victory

Principle 5: Voluntarily submit to every change God wants to make in my life and humbly ask Him to remove my character defects.

Happy are those whose greatest desire is to do what God requires.

Step 6: We were entirely ready to have God remove all these defects of character.

Humble yourselves before the Lord, and he will lift you up.

James 4:10

Step 7: We humbly asked Him to remove all our shortcomings.

If we confess our sins, he is faithful and will forgive us our sins and purify us from all unrighteousness.

1 John 1:9

Introduction

Tonight we are going to look at an overview of Principle 5. We are going to answer the question, How can you have victory over your defects of character?

Victory

We are going to use the acrostic VICTORY.

Voluntarily submit

Identify character defects

Change your mind

Turn over character defects

One day at a time

Recovery is a process

You must choose to change

The *V* is VOLUNTARILY submit to every change God wants me to make in my life and humbly ask Him to remove my shortcomings. The Bible says that we are to make an offering of our very selves to God. "Offer yourselves as a living sacrifice to God, dedicated to his service and pleasing to him. . . . Let God transform you inwardly by a complete change of your mind" (Romans 12:1–2 GNB).

When you accepted Principle 3, you made the most important decision of your life by choosing to turn your life over to God's will. That decision got you right with God; you accepted and determined to follow His Son Jesus Christ as your Lord and Savior.

Then you began to work on *you*. You made a fearless and moral inventory of yourself. The first step in any victory is to recognize the enemy. My inventory showed me that I was my greatest enemy.

You came clean by admitting and confessing to yourself, to God, and to another person your wrongs and your sins. For probably the first time in your life, you were able to take off the muddy glasses of denial and look at reality with a clear and clean focus.

Now you are considering what Step 6 says: that you are "entirely ready to have God remove all of your defects of character." You're at the place in your recovery where you say, "I don't want to live this way anymore. I want to get rid of my hurts, hang-ups, and habits. But how do I do it?"

The good news is that *you* don't do it!

Step 6 doesn't read, "You are entirely ready to have *you* remove all of your defects of character" does it? No, it says, "You are entirely ready to have *God* remove all your defects of character."

So how do you begin the process to have God make the positive changes in your life that you and He both desire?

You start by doing the *I* in victory: IDENTIFY which character defects you want to work on first. Go back to the wrongs, shortcomings, and sins you discovered in your inventory. Falling down doesn't make you a failure, staying down does! God just doesn't want us to admit our wrongs, He wants to make us right! He wants to give us a future and a hope! God just doesn't want to forgive us, He wants to change us! Ask God to first remove those character defects that are causing you the most pain. Be specific! "In his heart a man plans his course, but the LORD determines his steps" (Proverbs 16:9).

Let's move to the *C,* which stands for CHANGE your mind.

Second Corinthians 5:17 tells us that when you become a Christian, you are a new creation, a brand new person inside. The old nature is gone. The changes that are going to take place are the result of a team effort. Your responsibility is to take the action to follow God's direction for change. You have to let God transform (change) you by renewing your mind.

Let's look at Romans 12:2: "Do not conform any longer to the pattern of this world, but be transformed by the renewing of your mind. Then you will be able to test and approve what God's will is—his good, pleasing and perfect will."

To transform something means to change its condition, its nature, its function, and its identity. God wants to change more than just our behaviors. He wants to change the way we think. Simply changing behaviors is like trimming the weeds in a garden instead of removing them. Weeds always grow back unless they are pulled out by the roots. We need to let God transform our minds!

How? By the *T* in victory: TURNING your character defects over to Jesus Christ. Relying on your own willpower, your own self-will, has blocked your recovery. Your past efforts to change your hurts, hang-ups, and habits by yourself and were unsuccessful. But if you "humble yourselves before the Lord, . . . he will lift you up" (James 4:10).

Humility is not a bad word, and being humble doesn't mean you're weak. Humility is like underwear: we should have it, but we shouldn't let it show. Humility is to make the right estimate of one's self or to see ourselves as God sees us.

You can't proceed in your recovery until you turn your defects of character over to Jesus. Let go! Let God!

The next letter is *O:* ONE day at a time.

Your character defects were not developed overnight, so don't expect them to be instantly removed. Recovery happens *one day at a time!* Your lifelong hurts, hang-ups, and habits need to be worked on in twenty-four-hour increments. You've heard the old cliché: "Life by the yard is hard; life by the inch is a cinch." Jesus said the same thing: "So don't be anxious about tomorrow, God will take care of your tomorrow too. Live one day at a time" (Matthew 6:34 TLB).

When I start to regret the past or fear the future, I look to Exodus 3:14 where God tells us that His name is "I am."

I'm not sure who gets the credit for the following illustration, but it's right on. God tells me that when I live in the past with its mistakes and regrets, life is hard. I can take God back there to heal me, to forgive me, to forgive my sins. But God does not say, "My name is 'I was.'" God says, "My name is 'I am.'"

When I try to live in the future, with its unknown problems and fears, life is hard. I know God will be with me when that day comes. But God does not say, "My name is 'I will be.'" He says, "My name is I am."

When I live in today, this moment, one day at a time, life is not hard. God says, "I am here." "Come to me, all of you who are tired from carrying heavy loads, and I will give you rest" (Matthew 11:28).

Let's look at the letter *R:* RECOVERY is a process, "one day at a time" after "one day at a time."

Once you ask God to remove your character defects, you begin a journey that will lead you to new freedom from your past. Don't look for perfection, instead rejoice in steady progress. What you need to seek is "patient improvement." Hear these words of encouragement from God's Word: "And I am sure that God who began a good work within you will keep right on helping you grow in his grace until his task within you is finally finished on that day when Jesus Christ returns" (Philippians 1:6 TLB).

The last letter in victory is *Y:* YOU must choose to change.

As long as you place self-reliance first, a true reliance on Jesus Christ is impossible. You must voluntarily submit to every change God wants you to make in your life and humbly ask Him to remove your shortcomings. God is waiting to turn your weaknesses into strengths. All you need to do is *humbly ask!*

"God gives strength to the humble, . . . so give yourselves humbly to God. Resist the devil and he will flee from you. And when you draw close to God, God will draw close to you" (James 4:6–8 TLB).

Wrap-up

To make changes in our lives, all I had to do and all you need to do is to be *entirely* ready to let God be the life-changer. We are not the "how" and "when" committee. We are the preparation committee: all we have to be is *ready*!

Tonight, Jesus is asking you, "Do you want to be healed, do you want to change?" You must choose to change. That's what Principle 5 is all about! Let's close with prayer.

Dear God, show me Your will in working on my shortcomings. Help me not to resist the changes that You have planned for me. I need You to "direct my steps." Help me stay in today, not get dragged back into the past or lost in the future. I ask You to give me the power and the wisdom to make the very best I can out of today. In Christ's name I pray, AMEN.

PRINCIPLE 5 TESTIMONY

Hi, everyone, my name is Tom and Saddleback is my church family. I'm also a believer who struggled with alcoholism.

Actually, today I'm here to talk about my struggles with impatience, which, in my case anyway, always goes hand in hand with anger. Years ago I was honored with the prestigious title of "Angriest Man Alive." But today I'm here to share the hope and victory that is found in Christ.

Over the years, I've struggled at being patient with the irritations and inconveniences that we've all faced. But instead of learning to be patient, I watched my anger get more and more out of control until, finally, I lost everything.

Even at a young age, I remember anger being such a dominant factor in my life. With my four brothers and myself at home, there was this fear when my mother would erupt. I remember the one time I was saved from getting hit in the head with an iron. Thank God it was still plugged in and the cord wouldn't allow the iron to reach me. I'll tell you, I really just thought that was the way life was. Even being young and just in my teens, anger that came from anxiety dominated my thoughts and consequently my actions. In me burned a restlessness, an irrationality, and discontent. It caused such inner turmoil that I sought to drown out these feelings with alcohol and drugs. This was at the ripe old age of thirteen. As the storm raged in me, the only thing that would calm it was booze and drugs. See, to me, my drinking and drugging wasn't a problem—it was my solution. I just wanted the ease and comfort I saw in other peoples' lives. After awhile, impatience led to further anger and anger turned to rage.

By this time, in my early twenties, my outbursts had caused me to lose everything—jobs, family, a fiancée, and friends. I was left isolated, and again drugs and alcohol were my refuge. But still the rage grew and then turned inward. I had grown to hate the person I had become and dying seemed a welcome thing in my life. I remember calling my friend Matthew, one of the few friends who would still talk to me, and I said, "Matt, I'm tired and I just want to end it." He said, "Tom, can I ask you a question? Do you want to die, or do you just want to be happy?" Well, I thought, "Die . . . happy . . . die . . . happy." Hey, happy's not a bad choice! I just wanted peace.

Now, I had tried to get my act together before by making oaths and resolutions. But all these new moral codes and philosophies didn't work. You see, even with as much self-knowledge as I had, and even with all my human resources controlled by my will, I failed miserably. The needed power just wasn't there. Only an act of providence would save me.

That's when I sought help. I found a 12-Step recovery group and, in the process, found I needed God, which led me to the cross. Praise God! Praise God for Celebrate Recovery and this church. That's where I found my peace. It was kindness, mercy, and His grace that inspired me to turn to the Lord. Since I've given my life to the Lord, three things have happened.

First, I began to see life more and more from God's viewpoint. It's just a miracle how my whole perspective has changed. Just knowing He's in control sets me at ease. With less fear and anxiety, there's really no cause for anger. In Isaiah 41:10 His Word says, "Do not fear, for I am with you." Also, Philippians 4:7 talks about a peace that is beyond our understanding. This is not a peace I had in me, rather peace he put in me.

Second, God's love is replacing the anger in my life. Showing me I had value in His eyes, He demonstrated that love by dying on the cross for me. My response of love is to have faith that His ways are greater than my ways. And that trust has led to action. Through prayer, study of His Word, and walking in faith by His loving guidelines, He has transformed my mind and done for me what I could never have done for myself. And through His spirit, I've found the comfort that I've always looked for. He's turned my anxiety and despair to hope, my fear to faith, and my pain to compassion.

Finally, I'm depending every day on Christ to help me control my impatience. The peace I have only comes from having a totally dependent relationship with Jesus Christ. And I'm so glad my relationship is based on His faithfulness to me, not my faithfulness to Him.

You see, sometimes I still struggle with impatience. I started to lose my temper just yesterday, but I didn't react like the old angry Tom. Instead, I relied on His promises from 1 Thessalonians 5:23–24 and Philippians 1:6.

I'm not all I'd like to be, I'm not all that I could be, but praise God, I'm not the angry man I used to be. Thanks for letting me share.

Principle 6

Evaluate all my relationships. Offer forgiveness to those who have hurt me and make amends for harm I've done to others, except when to do so would harm them or others.

"Happy are the merciful" and *"Happy are the peacemakers."*

Amends

Principle 6: Evaluate all my relationships. Offer forgiveness to those who have hurt me and make amends for harm I've done to others, except when to do so would harm them or others.

Happy are the merciful.

Happy are the peacemakers.

Step 8: We made a list of all persons we had harmed and became willing to make amends to them all.

Do to others as you would have them do to you.

Luke 6:31

Introduction

This week, we are going to focus on Principle 6. In fact, we are going to spend the next two months on Principle 6. That's how important it is to our recovery. We will use some of the time for teaching and we will celebrate the Lord's Supper next week to help us really understand the true meaning of forgiveness, but I would like to use most of our time for testimonies from you. Please let me know if you would like to share your story of how Principle 6 has positively impacted your recovery and relationships.

Tonight, we are going to give an overview of Principle 6, which is all about making amends. "Forgive me as I learn to forgive" sums it up pretty well.

We started doing repair work on the *personal* side of our lives earlier in our recovery by admitting our powerlessness, turning our lives and wills over to God's care, doing our moral inventory, sharing our sins or wrongs with another, and admitting our shortcomings and asking God to remove them. But now we begin to do some repair work on the *relational* side of our lives. Making your amends is the beginning of the end of your isolation from God and others.

Still, some of us balk at making amends. We think, "If God has forgiven me, isn't that enough? Why should I drag up the past? After all, making amends doesn't sound natural."

The answer to that objection is simple: making amends is not about your *past* so much as it is about your *future*. Before you can have the healthy relationships that you desire, you need to clean out the guilt, shame, and pain that has caused many of your past relationships to fail.

So, in the words of Step 8, it is time to "make a list of persons that we have harmed and become *willing* to make amends to them all." At this point, you are only looking for the *willingness*. Step 8 only requires that we identify those to whom we need to make amends or offer forgiveness.

Luke 6:31 reminds us to treat others the way that you want to be treated. For some of you, that may be very difficult. You have been hurt very badly or abused. Many of you had nothing to do with the wrong committed against you.

Often I have counseled people on Principle 6 and on the critical importance of forgiveness, only to have them say, "Never will I forgive! Not after what was done to me!" In these cases, the wrong against the individual was often child molestation, sexual abuse, or adultery. Such sins are deep violations that leave painful wounds, but they also are the root of dysfunction that bring many people into recovery.

Forgiving the perpetrator of such wrongs, even after the one harmed has dealt with the emotional pain, seems impossible. We are going to deal specifically with this issue in the lesson on the three types of forgiveness.

For now, listen to the way Celebrate Recovery rewords this step for those in the sexual/physical abuse groups:

> Make a list of all persons who have harmed us and become willing to seek God's help in forgiving our perpetrators, as well as forgiving ourselves. Realize we've also harmed others and become willing to make amends to them.

Let's look at the second part of Principle 6: "... make amends for harm I've done to others, except when to do so would harm them or others."

Listen as I read Matthew 5:23–24: "Therefore, if you are offering your gift at the altar and there remember that your brother has something against you, leave your gift there in front of the altar. First go and be reconciled to your brother; then come and offer your gift."

The first part of Principle 6 deals with being willing to consider forgiveness. The second part of Principle 6 calls us to action as we make our amends and offer our forgiveness. Going back to the garden metaphor, we need to pull out the dead weeds in our past broken relationships so that we can clear a place where our new relationships can be successfully planted or restored. That's why Principle 6 is so important.

In Participant's Guide 3, on page 39 you will find the Amends list.

Column 1 is where you list the persons to whom you need to be willing to make amends, those whom you have harmed. Column 2 is for the persons that you need to become willing to forgive. List them this week.

During the next two months, add to them as God reveals to you others to include on your list. Remember, all you are doing at this point is writing them down.

Amends

Let's look at tonight's acrostic and answer the question, How do I make AMENDS?

Admit the hurt and the harm

Make a list

Encourage one another

Not for them

Do it at the right time

Start living the promises of recovery

The *A* is ADMIT the hurt and the harm. Principle 4 showed us how important it is to open up to God and to others. Your feelings have been bottled up far, far too long, and that has interfered with all your important relationships. In this step of your recovery you need to once again face the hurts, resentments, and wrongs others have caused you or that you have caused to others. Holding on to resentments not only blocks your recovery, it blocks God's forgiveness in your life.

Luke 6:37 (GNB) tells us, "Do not judge others, and God will not judge you; do not condemn others, and God will not condemn you; forgive others, and God will forgive you."

The next letter in amends is *M:* MAKE a list.

In addition to the amends worksheet in Participant's Guide 3, you will find the "Celebrate Recovery Inventory" in Participant's Guide 2. You can also use these sheets to help you make your amends list.

In column 1, on your inventory, you will find the list of people that you need to forgive. These are the people who have hurt you. In column 4, you will find the list of people to whom you owe amends. These are the ones whom you have hurt.

If it has been awhile since you did your inventory, God may have revealed others to you that you need to add to your list. That's why it's important to start off with the amends worksheet.

When you are making your list, don't worry about the "how-tos" in making your amends. Don't ask questions like *How could I ever ask my dad for forgiveness? How could I ever forgive my brother for what he did?* Go ahead and put the person on your list anyway. "Treat others as you want them to treat you" (Luke 6:31 TLB).

The *E* in amends stands for ENCOURAGE one another.

It has been said that encouragement is oxygen to the soul. Before you make your amends or offer your forgiveness to others, you need to have an accountability partner or a sponsor, someone to encourage you and to provide a good "sounding board." That person's objective opinion is valuable to insure that you make amends and offer forgiveness with the right motives.

Hebrews 10:24 says, "And let us consider how we may spur one another on toward love and good deeds." If you are asked to be an encourager, an accountability partner, or a sponsor, be honored. And remember, you can't hold a torch to light another's path without brightening your own.

The *N* in amends is the reason for making the amends: NOT for them.

You need to approach those to whom you are offering your forgiveness or amends humbly, honestly, sincerely, and willingly. Don't offer excuses or attempt to justify your actions; focus only on your part.

In five words, here's the secret to making successful amends: *Do not expect anything back!* You are making your amends, not for a reward, but for freedom from your hurts, hang-ups, and habits.

Principle 6 says that I am responsible to "make amends for harm I've done to others." Jesus said, "Love your enemies and do good to them; lend and expect nothing back" (Luke 6:35 GNB). God loves us generously and graciously, even when we are at our worst. God is kind; we need to be kind!

Do you know that you can become addicted to your bitterness, hatred, and revenge, just as you can become addicted to alcohol, drugs, and relationships? A life characterized by bitterness, resentment, and anger will kill you emotionally and shrivel your soul. They will produce the "Three Ds":

Depression

Despair

Discouragement

An unforgiving heart will cause you more pain and destruction than it will ever cause the person who hurt you.

Let's move on to the *D* in amends: DO it at the right time.

This principle not only requires courage, good judgment, and willingness, but a careful sense of *timing!*

Ecclesiastes 3:1 (TLB) tells us that "There is a right time for everything." There is a time to *let* things happen and a time to *make* things happen. There is a right time and a wrong time to offer forgiveness or to make amends.

Before making amends, you need to pray, asking Jesus Christ for His guidance, His direction, and His perfect timing.

Principle 6 goes on to say, ". . . except when to do so would harm them or others."

Listen to Philippians 2:4: "Each of you should look not only to your own interests, but also to the interests of others."

Don't wait until you *feel* like making your amends or offering your forgiveness; living this principle takes an act of the will! Or perhaps I should say a *crisis* of the will. Making your amends is an act of obedience to Scripture and of personal survival.

The last letter in amends is *S:* START living the promises of recovery.

> If we work this principle to the best of our ability, we will be amazed before we are halfway through, when we realize that we know a new freedom and a new happiness. We will no longer regret the past. We have a new understanding of serenity and peace. We will see how our experience with our hurts, hang-ups, and habits can benefit others.
>
> That feeling of uselessness and self-pity will disappear. We will lose interest in selfish things and gain interest in others, causing our self-seeking to slip away. Our whole attitude and outlook on life changes. And suddenly we realize that God is doing for us what we could not do for ourselves! (Paraphrased from the Big Book of AA, pages 83–84)

Wrap-up

Principle 6 offers you freedom—freedom from the chains of resentment, anger, and hurt; freedom, through your amends for the harm you caused others, to look them in the eye, knowing that you are working with God in cleaning up your side of the street.

In your small groups, I encourage those of you who have completed Principle 6 to share the freedom and the blessings that you have received.

Let's pray.

> *Dear God, I pray for willingness—willingness to evaluate all my past and current relationships. Please show me the people that I have hurt, and help me become willing to offer my amends to them. Also, God, give me Your strength to become willing to offer forgiveness to those that have hurt me. I pray for Your perfect timing for taking the action that Principle 6 calls for. I ask all these things in Your Son's name, AMEN.*

Forgiveness

Principle 6: Evaluate all my relationships. Offer forgiveness to those who have hurt me and make amends for harm I've done to others, except when to do so would harm them or others.

Happy are the merciful.

Happy are the peacemakers.

Step 8: We made a list of all persons we had harmed and became willing to make amends to them all.

Do to others as you would have them do to you.

Luke 6:31

Step 9: We made direct amends to such people whenever possible, except when to do so would injure them or others.

Therefore, if you are offering your gift at the altar and there remember that your brother has something against you, leave your gift there in front of the altar. First go and be reconciled to your brother; then come and offer your gift.

Matthew 5:23–24

Introduction

Tonight we are going to continue to work on evaluating all of our relationships. We will offer forgiveness to those who have hurt us and, when possible, make amends for the harm we've done to others, without expecting anything in return.

We have discussed how to make your amends, but tonight I would like to talk about something that can block, stall, or even destroy your recovery: the inability to accept and offer *forgiveness*.

I think we all agree that forgiveness is a beautiful idea until we have to practice it.

A guy once told me, "John, you won't catch me getting ulcers. I just take things as they come. I don't ever hold a grudge, not even against people who have done things to me that I'll never forgive." Right!

I saw this sign on a company bulletin board: "To err is human; to forgive is not company policy."

There are a lot of jokes about forgiveness, but forgiveness is not something that those of us in recovery can take lightly, because forgiveness is clearly God's prescription for the broken. No matter how great the offense or abuses, along the path to healing lies forgiveness.

We all know that one of the roots of compulsive behavior is pain—buried pain.

In Principle 1 we learned that pretending the hurt isn't there or that it doesn't bother you anymore won't solve your problems. Jeremiah 6:14 (TLB) reminds us that "You can't heal a wound by saying it's not there!"

Facing your past and forgiving yourself and those who have hurt you, and making amends for the pain that you have caused others is the only lasting solution. Forgiveness breaks the cycle! It doesn't settle all the questions of blame, justice, or fairness, but it does allow relationships to heal and possibly start over.

So tonight let's talk about the three kinds of forgiveness.

Forgiveness

In order to be completely free from your resentments, anger, fears, shame, and guilt, you need to give and accept *forgiveness* in all areas of your lives. If you do not, your recovery will be stalled and thus incomplete.

The first and most important forgiveness is extended from God to us. Have you accepted God's forgiveness? Have you accepted Jesus' work on the cross? By his death on the cross, all our sins were canceled, paid in full;

a free gift for those who believe in Him as the true and only Higher Power, Savior, and Lord.

Jesus exclaimed from the cross, "It is finished" (John 19:30). No matter how grievously we may have injured others or ourselves, the grace of God is always sufficient! His forgiveness is always complete!

Romans 3:22–25 (GNB) says, "God puts people right through their faith in Jesus Christ. God does this to all who believe in Christ, because there is no difference at all: everyone has sinned and is far away from God's saving presence. But by the free gift of God's grace all are put right with him through Jesus Christ, who sets them free. God offered him so that by his sacrificial death he should become the means by which people's sins are forgiven through their faith in him."

Remember, if God wasn't willing to forgive sin, heaven would be empty.

The second kind of forgiveness is extended from us to others. Have you forgiven others who have hurt you? This type of forgiveness is a process. You need to be willing to be willing, but to be truly free, you must let go of the pain of the past harm and abuse caused by others.

Forgiveness is all about letting go. Remember playing tug-of-war as a kid? As long as the people on each end of the rope are tugging, you have a war. You "let go of your end of the rope" when you forgive others. No matter how hard they may tug on their end, if you have released your end, the war is over. It is finished! But until you release it, you are a prisoner of war!

Think about who your anger is hurting most. I'll give you a hint. It's you! Forgiveness enables you to become fully freed from your anger and allows you to move forward positively in those relationships.

The Bible has a lot to say about forgiveness. Romans 12:17–18 says, "Do not repay anyone evil for evil. Be careful to do what is right in the eyes of everybody. If it is possible, as far as it depends on you, live at peace with everyone."

Causing an injury puts you *below* your enemy. Revenging an injury makes you *even* with him. Forgiving him sets you one *above* him. But more importantly, it sets you free!

By the way, on your list of "others to forgive," you might have forgotten about someone you may need to forgive: God. Yes, you heard me right. God.

God cannot and does not sin. His very nature is marked by perfect holiness in every attribute and action. God is perfect in love, mercy, and grace. But remember that He loved us so much that He gave us a free will. He didn't want us to be His puppets. He wanted us to love Him as our choice. You need to understand and believe that the harm others did to you was from their free will. It was their choice, not God's. It was *not* God's will. Once you understand "free will" you will understand that your anger toward God has been misplaced.

His promise is found in 1 Peter 5:10 (PHILLIPS): "After you have borne these sufferings a very little while, the God of all grace, who has called you to share in his eternal splendor through Christ, will himself make you whole and secure and strong."

If you have been the victim of sexual abuse, physical abuse, or childhood emotional abuse or neglect I am truly sorry for the pain you have suffered. I hurt with you. But you will not find the peace and freedom from your perpetrators until you are able to forgive them. Remember, forgiving them in no way excuses them for the harm they caused you, but it will release you from the power they have had over you. I have rewritten Steps 8 and 9 of the 12 Steps for you.

> Step 8. Make a list of all persons who have harmed us and become willing to seek God's help in forgiving our perpetrators, as well as forgiving ourselves. Realize we've also harmed others and become willing to make amends to them.

> Step 9. Extend forgiveness to ourselves and to others who have perpetrated against us, realizing this is an attitude of the heart, not always confrontation. Make direct amends, asking forgiveness from those people we have harmed, except when to do so would injure them or others.

To recap, we need to accept God's forgiveness by accepting what Jesus did for us on the cross, and we need to forgive and ask forgiveness of others. The last kind of forgiveness is perhaps the most difficult for us to extend.

We need to forgive ourselves. Have you forgiven yourself? You can forgive others, you can accept God's forgiveness, but you may feel the guilt and shame of your past is just too much to forgive.

This is what God wants to do with the darkness of your past: "Come, let's talk this over! says the Lord; no matter how deep the stain of your sins, I can take it out and make you as clean as freshly fallen snow. Even if you are stained as red as crimson, I can make you white as wool! If you will only let me help you" (Isaiah 1:18–19 TLB).

No matter how unloved or worthless you may feel, God loves you! Your feelings about yourself do not change His love for you one bit.

Let me ask you a question: If God Himself can forgive you, how can you withhold forgiveness from yourself? In fact, I believe that we must forgive ourselves before we can honestly forgive others. The first name on your amends list needs to be God, the second needs to be yours. Why?

The answer is found in Matthew 22:36–40, where Jesus was asked,

"Which is the most important command?" Jesus replied, "'Love the Lord your God with all your heart, soul, and mind.' This is the first and greatest commandment. The second most important is similar: 'Love your neighbor as much as you love yourself.'"

Now how can you love or forgive your neighbor, if you can't love or forgive yourself? If you have not forgiven yourself, your forgiveness to others may be superficial, incomplete, and done for the wrong motives.

Self-forgiveness is not a matter of assigning the blame to someone else and letting yourself off the hook. It's not a license for irresponsibility. It is simply an acknowledgment that you are human like everybody else and that you've reached the stage in your recovery where you are able to give yourself greater respect.

Wrap-up

As you take the necessary steps of forgiveness, you will discover that you are letting go of the guilt and shame. You'll be able to say, "I'm not perfect, but God and I are working on me. I still fall down, but with my Savior's help, I can get up, brush myself off, and try again.

We can say, "I forgive myself because God has already forgiven me, and with His help, I can forgive others."

When you forgive yourself, you don't change the past, but you sure do change the future!

Grace

Principle 6: Evaluate all my relationships. Offer forgiveness to those who have hurt me and make amends for harm I've done to others, except when to do so would harm them or others.

Happy are the merciful.

Happy are the peacemakers.

Step 9: Made direct amends to such people whenever possible, except when to do so would injure them or others.

Therefore, if you are offering your gift at the altar and there remember that your brother has something against you, leave your gift there in front of the altar. First go and be reconciled to your brother; then come and offer your gift.

Matthew 5:23–24

Introduction

Tonight, we are going to finish discussing Principle 6. We have talked about how to evaluate all our relationships, offer forgiveness to those who have hurt us, and make amends for the harm that we have done to others, when possible without expecting anything back.

As we grow as Christians and as we grow in our recovery, we want to follow the guidance and directions of Jesus Christ. As we get to know Him better, we want to model His teachings and model His ways. We want to become more like Him. Honestly, if we are going to implement Principle 6 to the best of our ability, we need to learn to model God's grace. But how?

Grace

The key verses of Celebrate Recovery are 2 Corinthians 12:9–10 (NCV): "But he said to me, 'My grace is enough for you. When you are weak, my power is made perfect in you.' So I am very happy to brag about my weaknesses. Then Christ's power can live in me. For this reason I am happy when I have weaknesses, insults, hard times, sufferings, and all kinds of troubles for Christ. Because when I am weak, then I am truly strong."

Celebrate Recovery is built on and centered in Christ's grace and love for each of us.

Let's look at tonight's acrostic: GRACE.

God's gift

Received by our faith

Accepted by God's love

Christ paid the price

Everlasting gift

The *G* in grace is GOD'S gift

Grace is a gift. Grace cannot be bought. It is freely given by God to you and me. When we offer (give) our amends and expect nothing back, that's a gift from us to those whom we have hurt.

Romans 3:24 (NCV) tells us, "All need to be made right with God by his grace, which is a free gift. They need to be made free from sin through Jesus Christ."

First Peter 1:13 (NCV) says, "Prepare your minds for service and have self-control. All your hope should be for the gift of grace that will be yours when Jesus Christ is shown to you."

If my relationship with God was dependent on my being perfect, I would have trouble relating to God most of the time. Thank God that my relationship with Him is built on His grace and love for me. He gives the strength to make the amends and offer the forgiveness that Principle 6 requires.

And how do we receive God's gift of grace? That's the *R* in grace: RECEIVED by our faith.

No matter how hard we may work, we cannot earn our way into heaven. Only by professing our faith in Jesus Christ as our Lord and Savior can we experience His grace and have eternal life.

Ephesians 2:8–9 says, "For it is by grace you have been saved, through faith—and this not from yourselves, it is the gift of God—not by works, so that no one can boast."

Let me share another verse with you. Philippians 3:9 (TLB) states, "No longer counting on being saved by being good enough or by obeying God's laws, but by trusting Christ to save me; for God's way of making us right with himself depends on faith—counting on Christ alone."

You and I tend to be more interested in what we do. God is more interested in what we are.

Romans 5:2 says of Jesus, "Through whom we have gained access by faith into this grace in which we now stand. And we rejoice in the hope of the glory of God."

Just a word of warning: Our walk needs to match our talk. Our beliefs and values are seen by others in our actions. And it is through our faith in Christ that we can find the strength and courage needed for us to take the action Principle 6 requires: making your amends and offering your forgiveness.

The next letter in grace is *A*. We are ACCEPTED by God's love.

God loved you and me while we were still out there sinning. Romans 5:8 says, "God demonstrates his own love for us in this: While we were still sinners, Christ died for us."

We can, in turn, love others because God first loved us. We can also forgive others because God first forgave us. Colossians 3:13 (TLB) says, "Be gentle and ready to forgive; never hold grudges. Remember, the Lord forgave you, so you must forgive others."

Ephesians 2:5 (NCV) reminds us that "Though we were spiritually dead because of the things we did against God, he gave us new life with Christ. You have been saved by God's grace."

I don't know about you, but I know that I do not deserve God's love. But the good news is He accepts me in spite of myself! He sees all my failures and loves me anyway. And the same goes for you.

Hebrews 4:16 (NCV) tells us, "Let us, then, feel very sure that we can come before God's throne where there is grace. There we can receive mercy and grace to help us when we need it."

Let's move on to the C in grace: CHRIST paid the price.

Jesus died on the cross so that all our sins, all our wrongs, are forgiven. He paid the price, sacrificed Himself for you and me so that we may be with Him forever.

When we accept Christ's work on the cross, we are made a new creation. We can then rely on God's strength and power to enable us to forgive those who have hurt us. We can set aside our selfishness and speak the truth in love. We focus only on our part in making amends or offering our forgiveness.

Ephesians 1:7 (NCV) says, "In Christ we are set free by the blood of his death, and so we have forgiveness of sins. How rich is God's grace."

The last letter in grace is E: God's grace is an EVERLASTING gift.

Once you have accepted Jesus Christ as your Savior and Lord, God's gift of grace is forever.

Let me read a quote from the Big Book of AA, pages 83–84: "Once you have completed Step Nine, you will know a new freedom and a new happiness. . . . you will comprehend the word serenity and know peace. . . . You will suddenly realize that God is doing for you what you could not do for yourself."

And here's a quote from the *real* Big Book—the Bible: "And I am sure that God who began the good work within you will keep right on helping you grow in his grace until his task within you is finally finished on that day when Jesus Christ returns" (Philippians 1:6 TLB).

Also, 2 Thessalonians 2:16 (NCV) states, "May our Lord Jesus Christ himself and God our Father encourage you and strengthen you in every good thing you do and say. God loved us, and through his grace he gave us a good hope and encouragement that continues forever."

My life verse is 1 Peter 2:9–10 (TLB), where God says, "For you have been chosen by God himself—you are priests of the King, you are holy and pure, you are God's very own—all this so that you may show to others how God called you out of the darkness into his wonderful light. Once you were less than nothing; now you [John Baker] are God's own. Once you knew very little of God's kindness; now your very lives have been changed by it."

I stand before you as a product of God's grace. Everyone here this evening who has let Christ into his or her life is also a product of God's grace. As we model this grace, we will be able to do the work that Principle 6 requires.

Let's close tonight with Colossians 1:6: "All over the world this gospel is bearing fruit and growing, just as it has been doing among you since the day you heard it and understood God's grace in all its truth."

PRINCIPLE 6 TESTIMONY

Hi, I'm Carl, and I'm here because the 12 Steps are an important part of my Christian life.

Before turning my life entirely over to God, my life was unmanageable. I finally hit bottom spiritually and admitted that I couldn't manage my own life. I asked Jesus Christ to manage it for me and be the Lord of my life. I sought God's plan for me, and through prayer, Bible study, and worship, I began to grow spiritually.

I knew that I still had a problem, but I didn't know exactly what, so last year I decided to check out Celebrate Recovery's 12-Step program. I immediately saw three steps that I really didn't want to do. The Fourth Step—a searching and fearless moral inventory of myself—required me to look at *all* my hurts, habits, and pain. Couldn't I just leave the past in the past? The Fifth Step, confessing the hang-ups, examining *all* of my relationships and resentments, and admitting the exact nature of *all* my wrongs to another person didn't sound too appealing either. Did I really have to tell them *everything*? But the Ninth Step—make direct amends to *all* the people I'd harmed, and offer forgiveness to those who'd hurt me—NO WAY did I want to do that!

I did, however, want to fix my character defects. "It works if you work it," my new friends in Celebrate Recovery told me, and Pastor John promised me that I would grow spiritually by working the 12 Steps. Because the 12 Steps are based on God's principles from the Bible, I made a commitment to work through the steps.

One of my new friends, a recovering addict, encouraged me to pray and ask Jesus Christ to walk through the 12 Steps with me, but not to pray this unless I was serious about it. My friend was gave me good advice; Jesus was with me as I worked through the steps, and we didn't take *any* shortcuts. He is faithful, and He still walks with me daily on my road to recovery.

I want to emphasize that I can't work this program without God's help. I can't do *any* of it without the power of my Higher Power, Jesus Christ.

I did my Fourth Step inventory, and God brought to my mind every person I had harmed or who had harmed me, and every resentment. I found myself listing *everybody*; family, friends, ex-girlfriends, coworkers. *Every* significant adult relationship I'd ever had. Looking back, I saw a past littered with wreckage I'd caused, a trail of people I'd damaged and hurt. And I carried resentments and plenty of my own emotional and spiritual scars. *Not* a pretty picture. Now I really dreaded the Ninth Step. But as I eagerly finished my Fifth Step confession, my sponsor assured me that when I got to the Ninth Step, I'd be just as eager to make those amends, and he was right.

In preparing my Eighth Step list, I let God guide me through prayer in listing *only* those persons to whom I needed to make amends. That list wasn't as long as my inventory, but it was long enough.

It was obvious to me why I needed forgiveness from most of the people on my list, but I didn't understand why I owed some of them an amends. After all, *they'd* hurt me, and even after a thorough inventory, I didn't see that I had hurt them in any way. At this point, I had to reconsider my Third and Eighth Steps: would I insist on *my* will and not list them, or would I submit to God's will, add their names to my list and be willing to make amends to them, even if I didn't understand why? I added their names to my list.

As I studied and memorized God's Word, I learned that forgiveness and reconciliation are really important. I must ask God for forgiveness, ask and offer forgiveness to others, and seek reconciliation. And it's *always* up to me to make the first move. I will never have to forgive anyone more than God has already forgiven me for my sins. And I will never have to do more than Jesus already did to reconcile me to God by dying on the cross for my sins. Colossians 3:13 tells us to "Bear with each other and forgive whatever grievances you may have against one another. Forgive as the Lord forgave you."

How do I forgive sins from the past? In my heart, I must forgive, and forgive, and forgive, and FORGIVE, whenever the hurt or resentment comes up, until it doesn't come up any more, as many times as it takes.

My sponsor gave me these helpful guidelines on making amends. First, explain the 12-Step program and why I'm making amends, that I'm doing this to get right with God. Second, focus on my part, and don't even mention their part. Third, tell them that I'm truly sorry for hurting them. Fourth, tell them that I'd like "the slate wiped clean." And fifth, don't expect anything from them in return. Explain the program, focus on my part, I'm truly sorry, wipe the slate clean, NO EXPECTATIONS.

Prayer is a very important part of all my steps, especially my amends. I would pray repeatedly for days before making my amends, asking God to help me love that person, and praying for that person. With one person, I started off literally praying through clenched teeth, "GOD, HELP ME TO LOVE HER." I discovered that I cannot sincerely pray for someone *and* continue to hold a resentment against that person. And prayer works.

Most of my amends involved asking for forgiveness. This can be very humbling. Promptly admitting when I'm wrong, has caused me to literally make U-turns to go back and make Tenth Step amends. Humbling, yes, but very necessary. For me the choice isn't whether to make amends or not make amends; it's whether to live in a healthy way or self-destruct. It's that simple.

Amends can be offering forgiveness. Several times, after I'd asked for forgiveness for what I'd done, the other person said, "Have I ever done anything to hurt you, because if I have, I'm not aware of it." This really surprised me at first, and I thought, "Are you kidding? You *really* hurt me! How could you *not* know?" At that moment God took control of me, and out of my mouth the words came quietly, "Let's just say that for whatever you've done to me, I forgive you, and the slate is clean for both of us." I didn't do that under *my own* power; that was God working in me. And God reminded me of what Jesus Christ said when they nailed Him on the cross: "Father, forgive them, for they know not what they are doing" (Luke 23:24).

Amends can be offering to make financial restitution. Once, God brought to my mind something I had done and lied about twenty years earlier that involved damaging someone else's property. I *really* didn't want to confess that lie, but again, back to the Eighth Step: was I willing to come clean? I confessed what I'd done, and offered to pay for the damage I'd caused.

Amends can be doing whatever it takes to try to restore a relationship, to make it right. After committing adultery, lying, and destroying my marriage, making amends to my wife included asking her, after years of separation, to trust enough to risk going with me to Christian marriage counseling. You see, God put it on my heart that *I* have to do everything *I* can to reconcile my marriage. Romans 12:18 says, "If it is possible, as far as it depends on you, live at peace with everyone."

For the trust I'd shattered to be restored, I had to show that I'd really changed. I had to wait for as long as it took. Why, Lord? Why am I waiting on a marriage I'd destroyed, on a love that had *died*? God reminded me that he *specializes* in resurrections. How long, Lord, how long do I have to wait? And He told me, simply and clearly, "Wait." First Corinthians 13 says, "Love is patient, . . . it . . . always hopes, always perseveres. Love never fails." Again, who's will was I following, and was I willing to do whatever it took to make this amends?

Did she see some change and repentance in me? Two days after hearing me publicly confess my sins to ten thousand people here at Saddleback, she agreed to go with me to counseling. My part now is to keep doing everything I can to restore that relationship. And I must continue to be willing to let God change me into the man and husband He wants me to be. For me, that includes working a *serious* program with my accountability partners to guard against sin. Thanks guys, you really make a big difference in my life.

And God told me, "I will *heal* your family."

But sometimes there is no way to make amends; to ask forgiveness, to make restitution, to reconcile. What if the person is not available to talk to? What if there's nothing I can possibly do to make amends? What if I've caused permanent damage? Or worse?

When I was in my early twenties, I got a woman pregnant. For my selfish reasons, we had the pregnancy aborted. Although I didn't know it at the time, God says that abortion is wrong, that it's a sin.

In my Fifth Step I confessed and repented for this sin, and received God's forgiveness, but *who* do I talk to to make amends for this? How can I make amends for taking my unborn child's life? What restitution can I offer for the life I took?

The answer is, there is no way to make amends, to repay my child for the life I took. So what can I do? God told me to write a letter, and after I wrote it, I asked God to read it to my child in heaven. I'm going to read part of it to you now.

Dear child:

As a part of my 12-Step recovery program, based on the Word of God our Father, found in the Bible, I have realized that I harmed you and must make amends. I want to make amends, but nothing I can do, think, or say can make amends for taking your life, for which I am guilty.

My child, I won't try to make hollow excuses or rationalize, but I will tell you that I was blind to God's truth at that time. It is only recently that I have been convicted that a child is a person and God's predestined creation at the moment of its conception and that to end that life intentionally is a sin. This truth is eternal, but I did not acknowledge it then; I do now.

I am guilty of this sin. I am sorry for what I did to harm you. I have asked God our Father for forgiveness for this sin. I have repented from this sin and my wrong way of thinking and will never do this again.

I know that I will see you in heaven.

Love,
Dad

Thanks for letting me share.

Principle 7

Reserve a daily time with God for self-examination, Bible reading, and prayer in order to know God and His will for my life and to gain the power to follow His will.

Crossroads

Principle 7: Reserve a daily time with God for self-examination, Bible reading, and prayer in order to know God and His will for my life and to gain the power to follow His will.

Step 10: We continued to take personal inventory and when we were wrong, promptly admitted it.

So, if you think you are standing firm, be careful that you don't fall!
1 Corinthians 10:12

Introduction

You have arrived at a very important junction. You have traveled a long road, which required facing your denial; surrendering your life to Jesus Christ; taking an honest look at your life; listing, confessing, and sharing all your wrongdoing; being humble enough to allow God to make major changes in you; becoming willing to forgive or make amends; offering your forgiveness to those that have hurt you; making amends for all the harm that you have caused to others ...

WOW! That's quite a journey! Not too long ago, most of us would have said that it was an impossible journey, that we could never have changed or grown so much, that we could never have done the work that the first six principles ask of us.

And we would be right. We could never have made it through by ourselves on our own power. In fact, the only reason we have made it this far is because we made a decision way back in Principle 3 to turn our lives and wills over to the care of God.

Jesus explains it this way in John 8:32: "You will know the truth, and the truth will set you free." Then in John 14:6 He defines Truth by saying, "I am the way and the truth and the life. No one comes to the Father except through me." We have been set free from our addictions and our obsessive/compulsive behaviors because of the "Truth" we have asked into our hearts, Jesus Christ.

Because of this life-changing decision you made, Jesus has come in—at your invitation—and rebuilt the foundation of your life! You will undoubtedly see major changes, if you haven't already!

Principle 7 and Step 10 are a crossroads of your recovery. It is not a place to stop and rest on past accomplishments. We need to thank God for getting us this far on our road to recovery, praise Him for the many victories over our hurts, hang-ups, and habits we have seen in working the first nine steps, but we also need to continue working the last three steps with the same devotion and enthusiasm that got us to this point in our recoveries.

First Corinthians 10:12 puts it this way: "So, if you think you are standing firm, be careful that you don't fall!"

Most recovery material refers to Steps 10 through 12 (Principles 7 and 8) as the "maintenance steps." I disagree with the use of the word "maintenance."

I believe that it is in these steps and principles that your recovery, your new way of living, really takes off, really bears the fruit of all the changes that God and you have been working on together.

It is in Principles 7 and 8 where you and I will live out our recoveries for the remainder of our time here on this earth—one day at a time! That's much, much more than "maintenance," folks!

Step Ten

As we begin to work Step 10[1], we will see that it is made up of three key parts.

[1]Please note that though Step 10 and Principle 7 differ somewhat in their focus, both point toward the same result: the character and image of Christ in our daily life. This chapter will emphasize the step more than the principle, but in no way do we intend to discount the many benefits of daily living Principle 7.

1. The *what:* "We continued to take personal inventory . . ."

2. The *why:* ". . . and when we were wrong . . ."

3. The *then what:* ". . . promptly admitted it."

Tonight we are going to spend a little time looking at each of these parts of Step 10. Of course, we need an acrostic. Tonight the word is TEN.

Take time to do a daily inventory

Evaluate the good and the bad

Need to admit our wrongs promptly

The *T* answers the "what" question: TAKE time to do a daily inventory.

To inventory something is simply to count it. Businesses take inventory all the time. Principle 7 reminds us to "reserve a daily time with God for self-examination, Bible reading, and prayer." This gives us quiet time to count the good and bad things we did during a particular period of time. Lamentations 3:40 exhorts us to "examine our ways and test them, and . . . return to the LORD."

We need to ask ourselves these questions:

• What good did I do today?

• In what areas did I blow it today?

• Did I do or say anything that hurt anyone today?

• Do I owe anyone amends?

• What did I learn from my actions today?

I do this on a daily basis. I reflect on my day to see if I harmed someone, acted or reacted out of fear or selfishness, or went out of my way to show kindness.

As we stressed in Principle 4, our daily inventories need to be balanced. We need to look at the things we did right as well as the areas in which we missed the mark and blew it! Believe it or not, by the time we get to Principle 7, we actually start doing a lot of things right. But if we are not careful, we can slowly slip back into our old habits, hang-ups, and dysfunctions, so we need to take regular, ongoing inventories.

The *E* in our acrostic answers the "why" question: EVALUATE the good and the bad.

The step doesn't say, " . . . *if* we're wrong." That's what I *wish* it said. *If* I'm ever wrong . . . *if* perhaps I blew it . . . No. The step says *when* I'm wrong.

Sometimes, I really do not want to work this step. If forces me to admit that, on a daily basis, I'm going to be wrong and I'm going to make mistakes. I struggled with this for years in my early recovery, until one day I saw a sign that was hanging in an AA meeting in downtown Los Angeles. The sign read: "Would you rather be right . . . or well?"

Would *you* rather be right or well?

First John 1:8–10 (TLB) says: "If we say we have no sin, we are only fooling ourselves, and refusing to accept the truth. But if we confess our sins to him, he can be depended on to forgive us and to cleanse us from every wrong. (And it is perfectly proper for God to do this for us because Christ died to wash away our sins). If we claim we have not sinned, we are lying and calling God a liar, *for he says we have sinned.*"

In John 3:21 Jesus tells us, "Whoever lives by the truth comes into the light." Step 10 brings us, on a daily basis, into the light.

Once we see the light, we have a choice. We can ignore it or we can act on it. If we act, we are living the last part of Step 10 and answer the "then what" question. We NEED to admit our wrongs promptly.

For years I couldn't admit it when I was wrong. My wife can vouch for that! I couldn't admit my mistakes. My refusal to offer amends blocked all my relationships, especially with my family. As I grew and matured in the Word and recovery, I discovered that I had to *own* my mistakes and take responsibility for my actions. I couldn't do that if I didn't take time daily to allow God to show me where I missed the mark.

There's another word that I wish had been left out of Step 10, the word "promptly." It's easier for me to admit the mistakes I made ten years ago than the mistakes I just made today. But Step 10 says promptly! As soon as I realize that I blew it I need to promptly admit it!

In Matthew 5:23–24 (THE MESSAGE), Jesus tells us, "This is how I want you to conduct yourself in these matters. If you enter your place of worship and, about to make an offering, you suddenly remember a grudge a friend has against you, abandon your offering, leave immediately, go to this friend and make things right. Then, and only then, come back and work things out with God."

In other words, admit your wrongs . . . promptly!

Wrap-up

One way to easily keep track of your good and bad behavior is to keep a journal. Participant's Guide 4 has space on pages 19–25 for you to practice using a journal for one week. Now, your journal is not for you to record the calories that you had for lunch today or your carpool schedule for school. Your journal is a tool for you to review and write down the good and the bad things you did today.

Look for negative patterns, issues that you are continually writing down and having to promptly make amends for—again and again. Share them with your sponsor or accountability partner, and set up an action plan for you, with God's help, to overcome them.

Try to keep your journal for seven days. Start out by writing down one thing that you are thankful for from your experiences from the day. That will get you writing.

If you haven't used a journal so far in your recovery, I believe you will find this recovery tool a great help!

Next week we will talk about the how-tos of Step 10 and ways of avoiding constantly needing to offer your amends.

Daily Inventory

Principle 7: Reserve a daily time with God for self-examination, Bible reading, and prayer in order to know God and His will for my life and to gain the power to follow His will.

Step 10: We continued to take personal inventory and when we were wrong, promptly admitted it.

So, if you think you are standing firm, be careful that you don't fall!
1 Corinthians 10:12

Introduction

Tonight we want to focus on the how-tos of Step 10. But first, I would like to see how you did with your seven days of Step 10 journaling. I know for many of you it was the first experience in writing down your thoughts on a daily basis. I thought it would be interesting to randomly call on some of you to come up here and read them for the whole group. Just kidding!

But, it is important to recap our day in written form—the good and the bad, the successes and the times when we blew it. Here's why:

1. When you write down areas in which you owe amends, it will help you see if patterns are developing, so you can identify them and work on them with the help of Jesus Christ and your sponsor.

2. You can keep the amends you owe to a very "short list." As soon as you write down an issue you can make a plan to PROMPTLY offer your amends. After you make the amends you can cross it off in your journal.

Inventory

Some of you may have had trouble getting started writing in your journal. Let me give you three hints that will help you get started putting the ink on the paper.

1. Last time we talked about starting off by writing down just one thing that happened that particular day for which we are thankful. Just one thing can get you started, and it will also help you sleep better that night.

2. Ask your accountability partner/sponsor to hold you accountable for writing in your journal each night.

3. This is the one that really works for me! Memorize Galatians 5:22–23, the "fruit of the Spirit": "The fruit of the Spirit is love, joy, peace, patience, kindness, goodness, faithfulness, gentleness and self-control."

Daily ask yourself any of these questions to prompt your writing, starting each question with the word "today":

- How did I show *love* to others?

- Did I act in an unloving way toward anyone?

- Did others see in me the *joy* of having a personal relationship with the Lord? If not, why not?

- How was my serenity, my *peace*? Did anything happen that caused me to lose it? What was my part in it?

- Was I *patient*? What caused me to lose my patience? Do I owe anyone amends?

- Would anyone say that I was *kind/good*? In what ways did I act unkind?

- How was my *faithfulness*?

- Did I keep my word with everyone?

- How was my *gentleness* and *self-control*? Did I lose my temper, speak a harsh or unkind word to someone?

As we work Step 10 and Principle 7, we begin the journey of applying what we have discovered in the first nine steps. We humbly live daily—in reality, not denial. We have done our best to amend our past. Through God's guidance, we can make choices about the emotions that affect our thinking and actions. We start to take action—positive action—instead of constant *reaction*.

In Principle 7 we desire to grow daily in our new relationship with Jesus Christ and others. Instead of attempting to be in control of every situation and every person we come in contact with, or spinning out of control ourselves, we are starting to exhibit self-control, the way God want us to be. Remember "self under control" is what we are seeking. Self under *God's* control is what we are striving for.

God has provided us with a daily checklist for our new lifestyle. It's called the "Great Commandment," and it is found in Matthew 22:37–40: Jesus said, "'Love the Lord your God with all your heart . . . soul and . . . mind.' This is the first and greatest commandment. And the second is like it: 'Love your neighbor as yourself.' All the Law and the Prophets hang on these two commandments."

When you do your daily personal inventory, ask yourself, "Today, did my actions show what the second greatest commandment tells me to do? Did I love my neighbor (others) as myself?"

As we live the two commandments by putting the principles and steps into action in our lives, we will become more like Christ. We will become doers of God's Word, not hearers only. James 1:22 says, "Do not merely listen to the word, and so deceive yourselves. Do what it says." Our actions need to be consistent with our talk. You may be the only Bible someone ever reads. That's being a real "Living Bible." That's how the apostle Paul lived. He says in 1 Thessalonians 1:5 (TLB), "Our very lives were further proof to you of the truth of our message." Others should see God's truth shown in our lives.

Step 10 does not say how often to take an inventory, but I would like to offer three suggestions that can help us keep on the right road, God's road to recovery.

Do an ongoing inventory

We can keep an ongoing inventory throughout the day. The best time to admit we are wrong is the exact time that we are made aware of it. Why wait? Let me give you an example.

Yesterday afternoon, I snapped at my son. I was immediately faced with a choice. I could admit that I was wrong ("I shouldn't have snapped at Johnny; all he wanted to do was play catch") and make amends with him ("Johnny, I'm sorry for speaking so sharply; I was wrong"), or I could wait until later and risk rationalizing it away ("He saw I was busy; he had no right to ask me to play at that time").

You don't have to wait until you go home, cook dinner, watch TV, and then start your journal. If you do an ongoing inventory during the day, you can keep your amends list very short!

Do a daily inventory

At the end of each day, we look over our daily activities, the good and the bad. We need to search where we might have harmed someone or where we acted out of anger or fear. But once again, remember to keep your daily inventory balanced. Be sure to include the things that you did right throughout the day. The best way to do this is to journal.

I spend about fifteen minutes just before I go to sleep, journaling my day's events, asking God to show me the wrongs that I have committed. Then, as promptly as I can the next morning, I admit them and make my amends.

Do a periodic inventory

I take a periodic inventory about every three months. I get away on a "mini retreat"! I would encourage you to try it. Bring your daily journal with you, and pray as you read through the last ninety days of your journal entries. Ask God to show you areas in your life that you can improve on in the next ninety days and *celebrate the victories* that you have made.

By taking an ongoing, a daily, and a periodic inventory we can work Step 10 to the best of our abilities. With God's help we can keep our side of the street clean.

Here are a few key verses to learn and follow for Step 10.

> Intelligent people think before they speak; what they say is then more persuasive.
>
> Proverbs 16:23 (GNB)

> Let no foul or polluting language, nor evil word, nor unwholesome or worthless talk (ever) come out of your mouth, but only such (speech) as is good and beneficial to the spiritual progress of others.
>
> Ephesians 4:29 (AMPLIFIED)

> A wise, mature person is known for his understanding. The more pleasant his words, the more persuasive he is.
>
> Proverbs 16:21 (GNB)

> A word of encouragement does wonders!
>
> Proverbs 12:25 (TLB)

> If I had the gift of being able to speak in other languages without learning them, and could speak in every language there is in all of heaven and earth, but didn't love others, I would only be making noise.
>
> 1 Corinthians 13:1 (TLB)

Step 10 daily action plan

1. Continue to take a daily inventory, and when you are wrong, promptly make your amends.

2. Summarize the events of your day in your journal.

3. Read and memorize one of the Principle 7a verses.

4. Work all steps and principles to the best of your ability.

The key verse for this lesson is Mark 14:38: "Watch and pray so that you do not fall into temptation. The spirit is willing, but the body is weak." Let's close in prayer.

> *Dear God, thank You for today. Thank You for giving me the tools to work my program and live my life differently, centered in Your will. Lord, help me to make my amends promptly and ask for forgiveness. In all my relationships today help me to do my part in making them healthy and growing. In Jesus' name I pray, AMEN.*

PRINCIPLE 7A TESTIMONY

My name is Rosanne and I am an alcoholic. I grew up in what I term a "dysfunctional family." My parents divorced when I was about six months old. I have two older brothers, an older sister, and a younger half-sister. We mostly lived with my mom in my youth. My father was always a practicing alcoholic up until about two years ago when he got sober. I do not blame either one of my parents for my alcoholism. Both of my parents were Jewish and raised us as such. I even had my Bat Mitzvah at the age of seventeen. They also both have been married four times, so we had a lot of parents running around our house. When I was ten years old, my mom decided to move us all to Lake Tahoe, where there weren't any drugs or alcohol. She was afraid for us kids. That's where I learned "wherever you go, there you are." You can't escape your problems. By age thirteen, I was smoking cigarettes and pot with my older siblings. Occasionally, I would do some other drugs. Alcohol did not become my drug of choice until about age sixteen. I hung around with the "good" kids, you know, the cheerleaders and football players, so I didn't think I'd have a problem. But by the age of twenty-one, I was a daily drinker. I was a blackout drinker and threw up every day. Every morning I would say, "I'll never drink again," and every night I was pouring the wine again. I just could not stop.

I ended up meeting and marrying another practicing alcoholic like me. Shortly after we married, I got pregnant. Fortunately, God shed His grace upon me during the time of my pregnancy and I only drank one glass of wine every Saturday night. To this day I know that was God, because I could never quit on my own for even a day. I started going to Al-Anon. I didn't feel a part of it, but I needed help. I thought my husband was the problem, not me. Once my son was born, my alcoholism really took off. I had been a daily drinker, only now it was worse.

After almost two years, I couldn't take it any more and I decided to leave my husband. Three weeks later, in my new apartment with my two-year-old son, I realized that I was the one with the problem. I was still going through the same amount of alcohol, having blackouts, and just wanting everything to change but not doing anything about it. I was living in hell! The alcohol turned on me, no longer my friend. I said and did things that I would never do in a sober state.

I finally was able to admit that I had a problem. I remembered the Al-Anon meeting and the AA meeting that was next door. I called AA and my journey really began. I was welcomed with open arms. In AA they talked about this "Higher Power" concept and told me that many called their Higher Power "God." Since I was Jewish and raised with a belief in God, I didn't have a problem with God. So I called my Higher Power God, too. Once I admitted I was powerless over my addiction and that my life had become unmanageable—and understood what that meant—I was able to start my recovery.

The next step, my sponsor told me, was "Come to believe that a power greater than myself would restore me to sanity." I learned through working Step 2 that if I keep the same behavior and expect different results, I am totally insane. But, if I go to Jesus Christ and ask Him to give me the courage and the strength and the willingness to change my behavior, then so will the results change. With everything that has happened to me in sobriety, if I had kept on drinking I would probably be dead by now. Fortunately, God had another plan. Since I've been sober (my first day of sobriety was March 1, 1987), I divorced my first husband and married my current husband, who is very different from my first husband. We met when I was three years sober. This leads me to believe that I did learn to look at what I had been doing, why it didn't work, and how to do things a new way. In fact, the only thing I really had to change in sobriety was *everything*.

I was given hope by working the second step. First, I came. Then, I came to. And, then I came to believe. Jesus Christ showered me with His grace even before I believed. With God's help, I had the willingness to change the things I could and He gave me the power to change them. I kept on hearing, "Don't quit before the miracle; it's right around the corner!" I believed and I still believe. I still have hope.

I have survived financial difficulties, getting married, having a second child, getting cancer, losing a job I had held for eight and a half years, finding a new job, and battling a potentially life-threatening liver disease. Through all that, I never had to drink because I was taught in Step 2 to change my behavior, that drinking or using drugs wouldn't make the situation better—just worse. I learned to "think through the drink."

My favorite verses in the Bible are Matthew 7:7–8 (GNB), which read, "Ask, and you will receive; seek, and you will find; knock, and the door will be opened to you. For everyone who asks will receive, and anyone who seeks will find, and the door will be opened to him who knocks."

This verse really brings me to Step 10: "We continued to take a personal inventory and when we were wrong, promptly admitted it." Every day, I not only ask God for His blessing, but I also ask Him to show me where I have wronged Him or others, so that I may make amends and change my behavior. I learned that there are two parts to making amends. The first part is to acknowledge the wrong you've done and the second (and most important) part is to change your behavior. There are days when this step is very difficult to do, but I always ask the Lord to give me the courage to see the real me, as He and others see me. The actual prayer I use is "Search me, O God, and know my heart; test me and know my anxious thoughts. See if there is any offensive way in me, and lead me in the way everlasting" (Psalm 139:23–24).

While I was working on the eleventh step, "Sought through prayer and meditation to improve my conscious contact with God, praying only for knowledge of His will for me and power to carry that out," I became a Christian and received Jesus Christ as my Lord and Savior. But, that's another whole testimony . . .

Now, my husband, kids, and I all are members at Saddleback. My husband works in the Adventure Land Ministry with the two-year-olds on Sunday mornings and I have been involved in the high school ministry. At one point I was feeling just as uncomfortable on Sunday mornings with the kids as I had felt in high school. I went to my lead staff member and told her I didn't know if I could continue in the high school ministry. We talked about my "passion," which is recovery. She asked me to think about starting a ministry for high school kids that aren't necessarily addicts or alcoholics yet, but may be headed that way. I prayed a lot about it. The name came (I love acronyms)— TNT. It stands for a couple of things. First, Teens 'n' Temptation. The temptation could be cigarettes, sex, alcohol, drugs, even food. The problem is the same and the recovery process is the same. I want to help kids catch recovery before they hurt themselves and others too badly. The other meaning of TNT, of course, is that it's truly a "dynamite" ministry in this church for kids. We'll take them as young as they're being tempted, but they must not be older than high school age. I'm grateful to the Lord for giving me this opportunity. Please pray for me and all the kids.

Thank you for listening and for the opportunity to share with you.

Relapse

Principle 7: Reserve a daily time with God for self-examination, Bible reading, and prayer in order to know God and His will for my life and to gain the power to follow His will.

Step 11: Sought through prayer and meditation to improve our conscious contact with God, praying only for knowledge of His will for us and power to carry that out.

Let the word of Christ dwell in you richly.

Colossians 3:16

Introduction

(Note: At Saddleback Church, we start with Lesson 1 in January. Therefore, we are teaching Principle 7 in November. That's why this lesson begins with a reference to Christmas.)

Tonight, we are going to start working on Principle 7. We are going to look specifically at how to maintain the momentum of your recovery during the approaching holidays!

Holidays can be tough, especially if you are alone, or if you are still hoping your family will live up to your expectations. This is a key time of the year to guard against slipping back to your old hurts, hang-ups, or habits. A key time to guard against relapse!

Therefore, tonight we are going to talk about how you can prevent RELAPSE. You don't have to start your Christmas shopping yet, but it's not too early to start working on a relapse-prevention program.

Preventing Relapse

Tonight's acrostic is RELAPSE:

Reserve a daily quiet time

Evaluate

Listen to Jesus

Alone and quiet time

Plug in to God's power

Slow down

Enjoy your growth

The first letter in relapse stands for Principle 7 itself: RESERVE a daily quiet time with God for self-examination, Bible reading, and prayer in order to know God and His will for my life and gain the power to follow His will.

As I said, during the holidays, it's easy to slip back into our old hurts, hang-ups, and habits. The alcoholic goes back to drinking, the overeater gains the weight back, the gambler goes back to "loss wages" (Las Vegas), the workaholic fills up his schedule, the codependent goes back to an unhealthy relationship. The list goes on and on.

The first step in preventing a relapse is to admit that you will be tempted, that you are not above temptation. Jesus wasn't, why should you be?

We find the account of Jesus' temptation in Matthew 4:1–11 (TLB):

> Jesus was led out into the wilderness to be tempted there by Satan.... For forty days and forty nights he ate nothing and became very hungry. Then Satan tempted him to get food by changing stones into loaves of bread.
> "It will prove you are the Son of God," he said.
> But Jesus told him, "No! For the Scriptures tell us that bread won't feed men's souls: obedience to every word of God is what we need."
> Then Satan took him to Jerusalem to the roof of the Temple. "Jump off," he said, "and prove you are the Son of God."
> Jesus retorted, "It also says not to put the Lord your God to a foolish test."
> Next, Satan took him to the peak of a very high mountain and showed him the nations of the world and all their glory. "I'll give it all to you," he said, "if you will only kneel and worship me."

"Get out of here, Satan. . . . The Scriptures say, 'Worship only the Lord God. Obey only him.'"

Then Satan went away, and angels came and cared for Jesus.

The test was over; the devil left. Jesus was tempted. He never sinned, but He was tempted.

Mark 14:38 tells us all to "Watch and pray so that you will not fall into temptation. The spirit is willing, but the body is weak."

Remember, being tempted isn't a sin. It's falling into the action of the temptation that gets us into trouble. You know it's odd, temptations are different from opportunities. Temptations will always give you a second chance!

Temptation is not a sin; it is a call to battle. When we are tempted to fall back into our old hurts, hang-ups, and habits we need to do as Jesus did in Matthew 4:10 (TLB): "'Get out of here, Satan,' Jesus told him. 'The Scriptures say, "Worship only the Lord God. Obey only him."'"

The next word in our acrostic reminds us of Step 10: EVALUATE.

Let me just recap what we have talked about in the last two lessons. Your evaluation needs to include your physical, emotional, relational, and spiritual health.

As Pastor Rick (Warren) says, don't forget the value of doing a "H-E-A-R-T" check. Ask yourself daily if you are

Hurting

Exhausted

Angry

Resentful

Tense

If you answer yes to any of the above, just use the tools you have learned in recovery to help get you back on track. We find specific instructions for this step in Romans 12:3–17: "Be honest in your estimate of yourselves. . . . Hate what is wrong. Stand on the side of the good. Love each other. . . . Be patient in trouble. . . . Do things in such a way that everyone can see you are honest clear through."

Daily practice of Step 10 maintains your honesty and humility.

The *L* is LISTEN to your Higher Power, Jesus Christ.

We need to take a time out from the world's "rat race" long enough to listen to our bodies, our minds, and our souls. We need to slow down enough to hear the Lord's directions. "Test everything that is said to be sure it is true, and if it is, then accept it" (1 Thessalonians 5:21 TLB). I like that verse in *The Message:* "Don't be gullible." Check out everything and keep only what's good. Throw out anything tainted with evil.

Let's look at the letter *A*, which stands for ALONE and quiet time.

The first part of Step 11 says: "We sought through prayer and meditation to improve our conscious contact with God."

In Principle 3, we made a decision to turn our lives and our wills over to God's care; in Principle 4, we confessed our sins to Him; and in Principle 5, we humbly asked Him to remove our shortcomings.

Now, in Principle 7 in order to keep your recovery growing, you need to have a daily quiet time with Jesus. Even He spent time alone with His Father; you need to do the same. Set a daily appointment time to be alone with God, so that you can learn to listen carefully, learn how to hear God!

In Psalm 46:10 God tells us to "Be still, and know that I am God."

Step 11 uses the word "meditation." Meditation may be new to you, and you may feel uncomfortable. The definition of meditation is simply "slowing down long enough to hear God." With practice, you will begin to realize the value of spending time alone with God.

The Enemy will use whatever he can to disrupt your quiet time with God. He will allow you to fill your schedule with so many good things that you burn out or do not have the time to keep your appointment with God. The Enemy loves it when he keeps us from growing and from working on the most important relationship in our lives—our relationship with Jesus.

Psalm 1:1–3 (GNB) tells us that: "Happy are those who . . . find joy in obeying the Law of the Lord, . . . they study it day and night. They are like trees that grow beside a stream, that bear fruit at the right time."

The next letter is *P:* PLUG in to God's power through prayer.

I can't tell you the number of people who, in counseling, have asked me, "Why did God allow that to happen to me?"

I reply, "Did you pray and seek His will and guidance before you made the decision to get married, before you made the decision to change jobs?" or whatever their issue might be.

You see, if we don't daily seek His will for our lives, how can we blame Him when things go wrong?

Some people think their job is to give God instructions. They have it backwards. Our job is to daily seek His will for our lives. You see, God's guidance and direction can only start when our demands stop.

Don't misunderstand me here. I'm only suggesting that we must stop *demanding* things of God, not stop *asking* things of Him. Specific prayer requests are another way to be plugged into God's power.

In Philippians 4:6, Paul tells us to pray about everything asking for God's perfect will in all our decisions: "Don't worry about anything; instead, pray about everything; tell God your needs and don't forget to thank him for his answers."

The verse says *His* answers, *His* perfect will—not mine or yours. Ours are imperfect and most often self-centered. We often use prayer as a labor-saving device, but I need to remind myself daily that God will not do for me what I can do for myself. Neither will God do for you what you can do for yourself.

Let's look at the *S* in our acrostic: SLOW down long enough to hear God.

After you spend time alone with God, you need slow down long enough to hear His answers and direction. After we pray and ask, we need to listen. God said to Job, "Listen to me. Keep silence and I will teach you wisdom!" (33:33 TLB).

Philippians 4:7 (TLB) tells us: "If you do this [present your requests to God] you will experience God's peace, which is far more wonderful than the human mind can understand. His peace will keep your thoughts and your hearts quiet and at rest as you trust in Christ Jesus."

Finally, the last letter in relapse is *E:* ENJOY your growth.

You need to enjoy your victories. Rejoice in and celebrate the small successes along your road to recovery! First Thessalonians 5:16 (GNB) tells us to "be joyful always, pray at all times, be thankful in all circumstances. This is what God wants from you in your life in union with Christ Jesus." And don't forget to share your victories, no matter how small, with others in your group. Your growth will give others hope!

With daily practice of these principles and with Christ's loving presence in your life, you will be able to maintain and continue to grow in recovery!

Wrap-up

Honestly, sometimes I wish I could take a vacation from my recovery, especially during the holidays. I'm sure you all have felt that way at one time or another. But let me assure you that relapse is real. It does happen! And it can be very costly. I urge you to take the actions that we talked about tonight to prevent relapse.

Let's get practical. Here are some things to do to prevent relapse during the holidays:

1. Pray and read your Bible daily. Establish a specific time of day to have your "quiet time."

2. Make attending your recovery meeting a priority. Stay close to your support team. If you find yourself saying, "I'm too busy to go to Celebrate Recovery tonight," make time. Flee from whatever you are doing and come share your recovery.

3. Spend time with your family if they are safe. If they are not, spend time with your church family. We are going to have Celebrate Recovery every Friday night throughout the holidays. You do not have to be alone this holiday season.

4. Get involved in service. Volunteer! You don't have to wait until you get to Principle 8 to start serving.

These are just a few ideas and suggestions. Share tonight in your small groups on ways that you, with God's help, can prevent relapse in your recovery.

Gratitude

Principle 7: Reserve a daily time with God for self-examination, Bible reading, and prayer in order to know God and His will for my life and to gain the power to follow His will.

Step 11: We sought through prayer and meditation to improve our conscious contact with God, praying only for knowledge of His will for us and power to carry that out.

Let the word of Christ dwell in you richly.

Colossians 3:16

Introduction

Tonight we are going to focus our attention outward rather than inward. We have taken many steps on our road to recovery. Our first step was to admit that we were (and are) powerless. Our second step led us to choose, once and for all, a power by which to live. We took our third and most important step when we chose to turn our lives and wills over to the only true Higher Power, Jesus Christ.

As we continue our journey, we grow in our conscious contact with God and He begins to unfold in our lives. And, as we begin to grow in our understanding of Him, we begin to live out the decision we made in Principle 3. We keep walking now, in peace, as we maintain inventories on a regular basis and as we continue to deepen our relationship with Christ. The way we do this according to Principle 7, is to "reserve a daily time with God." During this time we focus on Him by praying and meditating.

Prayer is talking to God. Meditation is listening to God on a daily basis. When I meditate I don't get into some yoga-type position or murmur, "om, om, om." I simply focus on and think about God or a certain Scripture verse or maybe even just one or two words. This morning I spent ten or fifteen minutes just trying to focus on one word: "gratitude."

I need to meditate every morning, but I don't. Some mornings my mind wanders and I find it very difficult to concentrate. Those old familiar friends will come back. You know, that old familiar committee of past dysfunction. The committee will try to do every thing it can to interrupt my quiet time with God. Through daily working the principles to the best of my ability, however, I've learned to shut them up most of the time.

I've learned to listen to God, who tells me that I have great worth. And He will say the same to you—if you will listen.

When I start my day with Principle 7 and end it by doing my daily inventory, I have a pretty good day—a reasonably happy day. This is one way I choose to live "one day at a time" and one way I can prevent relapse.

Another way to prevent relapse, especially during the holidays, is by maintaining an attitude of gratitude.

Gratitude

This week, the week before we celebrate Thanksgiving, I suggest that your prayers be focused on your gratitude in four areas of your life: toward God, others, your recovery, and your church. I'm going to ask you to write them down on your "gratitude list." This is an interactive lesson

We are going to take some time now for you to build your gratitude list for this Thanksgiving.

First, for what are you thankful to *God*? Offer prayers of gratitude to your Creator.

In Philippians 4:6, we're told, "Do not be anxious about anything, but in everything, by prayer and petition, with thanksgiving, present your requests to God."

Psalm 107:15 encourages us to "give thanks to the LORD for his unfailing love and wonderful deeds for men." What wonderful deeds they are! What are at least two areas of your life in which you can see God's work and that you are thankful for this holiday season?

You can reflect on the last eleven months or on what God has done for you this week or even today. Then take a moment to list just a few of the special things for which you are thankful to your Higher Power.

The next area is to list the individuals that God has placed in your life to walk alongside you on your road of recovery. We need to be thankful for *others*.

"Let the peace of Christ keep you in tune with each other, in step with each other. None of this going off and doing your own thing. And cultivate thankfulness. Let the word of Christ—the message—have the run of the house" (Colossians 3:15–16 THE MESSAGE).

Who are you thankful for? Why? Take a moment to list them.

The third area we can be thankful for is our *recovery*.

"As for us, we have this large crowd of witnesses around us. So then, let us rid ourselves of everything that gets in the way, and the sin which holds on to us so tightly, and let us run with determination the race that lies before us" (Hebrews 12:1 GNB).

What are two recent growth areas of your recovery for which you are thankful? Again, list them now.

The fourth and final area to be thankful for is your *church*.

"Enter the Temple gates with thanksgiving" (Psalm 100:4 GNB).

What are two things for which you are thankful to your church?

Wrap-up

Take your "gratitude list" home with you tonight and put it in a place where you will see it often. It will remind you that you have made progress in your recovery and that you are not alone, that Jesus Christ is always with you.

Using your gratitude list, going to your recovery meetings and making them a priority, getting involved in service in your church are the best way I know to prevent relapse during the holidays.

Let's close in prayer.

Dear God, help me set aside all the hassles and noise of the world to focus and listen just to You for the next few minutes. Help me get to know You better. Help me to better understand Your plan, Your purpose for my life. Father, help me live within today, seeking Your will and living this day as You would have me.

It is my prayer to have others see me as Yours; not just in my words but more importantly, in my actions. Thank You for Your love, Your grace, Your perfect forgiveness. Thank You for all those You have placed in my life, for my program, my recovery, and my church family. Your will be done, not mine. In Your Son's name I pray, AMEN.

PRINCIPLE 7B TESTIMONY

My name is Brett and I am a believer in Christ who struggles with issues commonly shared by children of alcoholics and other addicts.

I grew up in a rural community in the heartland of America. My parents were farmers throughout the majority of their adolescent and adult years. As a result, a strong, almost compulsive, work ethic was ingrained in the family. Unfortunately, another component was introduced into this family dynamic as well. I am not sure if initially this component was added to aid in relaxation, to help forget about a multitude of heartaches and setbacks associated with the farm, or to simply be a portion of the social setting after a hard day's work. I do know that the alcohol grew to become a substitute for interaction with the family members, to block intimacy in communication, and to anesthetize the pain and disappointments of life.

Looking back, I believe my dad often had a drink to break away from the perfectionism and performance issues that nagged at him as a result of growing up as the youngest child in a single-parent home with his father and four sisters. Even though I only spent my first four years on the farm, the behavior from that environment continued to manifest itself in our next residence. Oftentimes, when people hear the term "alcoholic" they think of a person who misses work and is passed out with a brown bag in his or her hand. On the contrary, my alcoholic parent was quite functional, never missed work, and was very financially responsible.

The primary issue was that Dad would either check out emotionally or become easily agitated when he would drink. I can clearly remember the sound of Dad's opening the refrigerator door in the basement, knowing that the next action would be the consumption of a shot or two of whiskey, directly off the bottle, followed by a beer. The audible cues signaled that it was time to give Dad his space—and plenty of it—to avoid conflict at any cost and to keep him happy. The result would translate into what I thought was a normal evening. Mom made every effort to run interference and to help avoid conflict. At the same time, however, she enabled Dad's behavior.

As the years passed, I did everything I knew to please others, avoid conflict, and excel to receive recognition. I was a member of many clubs in high school and college, received honors, awards, grades, and so forth, but I was never content. This performance-oriented behavior continued into my professional life as my career took off. However, the motivation for my success was not healthy. I was still trying to continue to please an unpleaseable parent even beyond the years of his life on earth.

During my years of scholastic and professional success, I egotistically took all the credit. It never crossed my mind that all of my talents, health, capabilities, and so forth were a gift from God. I did not realize they were a gift until I began to abuse and, to a degree, lose them. You see, even though work and school came easily, I always, always struggled with relationships.

During my second marriage, I was having a very difficult time with my stepdaughter. I was not sensitive to her needs, nor did I provide time for her. I visited a therapist and came to understand the issues were tied to my background as an ACA.

Five years of therapy helped my understanding academically, but in the deepest parts of my soul I knew something was missing . . . but I couldn't understand what. About that same time my wife, Cindi, suggested that we attend Saddleback Easter services at Trabuco Hills High School. Reluctantly, I agreed and continued to visit for the next two months. At the end of each service I would argue with Cindi about the message and its content. I was not about to succumb to admitting that I needed God. I was convinced I could handle anything the world could dole out. Meanwhile, my life went into a tailspin. I could no longer juggle the spinning plates; my stepparenting skills failed, I had pneumonia for three months, we were pinched financially, and I was stressed out about my job.

During a Sunday service about this time a new pastor was introduced who was leading a recovery ministry. At that moment I was convicted even deeper by God that I had been on the wrong path. I met John Baker and started my next five years with Celebrate Recovery. This time Christ was my Higher Power. I worked the steps as diligently, and if the truth be known, as compulsively as my little ACA legs would carry me. Seriously though, as I worked the steps, layers of hidden issues slowly began to be peeled back to reveal more to me. As I proceeded through the steps I reached Step 11, the step that reads, "We sought through prayer and meditation to improve our conscious contact with God, praying only for knowledge of His will for us and power to carry that out." The eleventh step was the fuel I needed to accept two things. First, that God would provide the peace and means to guide me and help me accept that my recovery is a lifelong process; and secondly, that He would always be there for me to talk to, to listen to, to be loved by, and to love back. All of these concepts were difficult for me because all of my life I was trying to *earn* things—approval, recognition, trust, forgiveness, and so forth. This step provided all of those things and more as long as I was obedient to have conscious contact with God.

As I took spiritual maturity classes at Saddleback, I came to understand that a daily quiet time was important if I was to grow in my relationship with my Higher Power, Jesus Christ. By reading God's Word and spending time in prayer, my intimacy with and understanding of His will became more clear. I began to claim that I am His child, that He loves me unconditionally, that I am forgiven, and that I cannot earn His love.

Working Step 11 also has helped me to develop patience, because God is teaching me to be still and listen, to wait on Him and to trust that He will provide *all* my needs. He helps me to know that I need to let go of my will and to seek out His will—that He is in control and I'm not. What a relief! In the quiet, still moments He helps me see all the things that have happened in my life to bring me to this moment today with you. I never knew He was so near and that I was so far away until I began to work the eleventh step. It is my prayer that each of you will continue with this step that is challenged by all of the barking dogs, doorbells, errands, wandering thoughts, and diversions that the world places in our way. Throughout this step I have come to claim Philippians 4:13 (NCV) as my life verse: "I can do all things through Christ, because he gives me strength." May you also allow Him to strengthen you.

Principle 8

Yield myself to God to be used to bring this Good News to others, both by my example and by my words.

"Happy are those who are persecuted because they do what God requires."

Give

Principle 8: Yield myself to God to be used to bring this Good News to others, both by my example and by my words.

Happy are those who are persecuted because they do what God requires.

Step 12: Having had a spiritual experience as the result of these steps, we try to carry this message to others and to practice these principles in all our affairs.

Brothers, if someone is caught in a sin, you who are spiritual should restore him gently. But watch yourself, or you also may be tempted.

Galatians 6:1

Introduction

I think that if God had to choose his favorite principle, He would choose Principle 8: "Yield myself to God to be used to bring this Good News to others, both by my example and by my words."

Why do I think Principle 8 is God's favorite? Because it is putting our faith into action. God's Word tells us in James 2:17, "Faith by itself, if it is not accompanied by action, is dead." Active faith is important to God!

Don't get me wrong, works are not going to save you. Only faith in Jesus Christ as your Lord and Savior can do that. It is through our actions, however, that we demonstrate to God and others the commitment we have to our faith in Jesus Christ.

So tonight, we are going to begin to work on Principle 8. In AA they call the corresponding step, Step 12, the "carrying the message" step, the "giving back" step.

What is "giving back" all about? What does it truly mean to give?

To answer that question, I did a word study on the meaning of "give" or "giving." In the New Testament, the word "give" has seventeen different Hebrew words with seventeen different meanings. So tonight, I thought you would find it interesting for me to do a thirty-minute lecture on each of the uses of the word "give." Just kidding!

Perhaps we'll take a more practical look at the meaning of the word "give" as it relates to Principle 8, since that's what this principle is really all about.

Principle 8 does not tell us to give in unhealthy ways, ways that would hurt us or cause us to relapse into our codependent behaviors. No, Principle 8 is talking about healthy, non-codependent giving of oneself without the slightest trace of expecting to receive back. Remember, no person has ever been honored for what they have received. Honor has always been a reward for what someone gave.

Matthew 10:8 sums up Principle 8: "Freely you have received, freely give."

In Principle 8, we *yield* ourselves to be used by God to bring this good news to others, both by our example and our words.

Give

It is in Principle 8 we learn what it means to truly GIVE.

God first

I becomes we

Victories shared

Example of your actions

The *G* stands for GOD first.

When you place God first in your life, you realize that everything you have is a gift from Him. You realize that your recovery is not dependent or based on material things, it is built upon your faith and your desire to follow Jesus Christ's direction.

Romans 8:32 (GNB) says that God "did not even keep back his own Son, but offered him for us all! He gave us his Son—will he not also freely give us all things?"

We are never more like God than when we give—not just money or things but our very selves. That's what Jesus did for us. He gave us the greatest gift of all—Himself.

The second letter in give is *I*. When we give, the I becomes we.

None of the steps or principles begin with the word "I." The very first word in Step 1 is "we." In fact, the word *we* appears in the 12 Steps fourteen times. The word "I" never appears even once in any of the 12 Steps. The road to recovery is not meant to be traveled alone. This is not a program to be worked in isolation.

Jesus said, "'Love the Lord your God with all your heart and with all your soul and with all your mind.' This is the first and greatest commandment. And the second is like it: 'Love your neighbor as yourself'" (Matthew 22:37–39).

When you have reached this step in your recovery and someone asks you to be a sponsor or to be an accountability partner, do it! The rewards are great, and sponsorship is one way to carry the message!

Ecclesiastes 4:9–12 (GNB) makes this concept of giving very clear: "Two are better off than one, because together they can work more effectively. If one of them falls down, the other can help him up. But if someone is alone . . . there is no one there to help him. . . . Two men can resist an attack that would defeat one man alone."

The third letter stands for VICTORIES shared.

God never, never, never, ever wastes a hurt! He can take our hurts and use them to help others. Principle 8 gives us the opportunity to share our experiences, strengths, and hopes with one another.

Deuteronomy 11:2 tells us to remember what we've learned about the Lord through our experiences with Him. We start off by saying, "This is how it was for me; this is the *experience* of what happened to me. This is how I gained the *strength* to begin my recovery, and there's *hope* for you."

Second Corinthians 1:3 (GNB) encourages us to "give thanks to the God and Father of our Lord Jesus Christ, the merciful Father, the God from whom all help comes! He helps us in all our troubles, so that we are able to help others who have all kinds of troubles, using the same help that we ourselves have received from God."

All the pain, all the hurt that my twenty years of abusing alcohol caused, all the destruction that I caused to myself and those I loved, finally made sense when I got to Principle 8. I finally understood Romans 8:28 (TLB): "We know that all that happens to us is working for our good if we love God and are fitting into his plans."

He called me according to His plans, and because I answered God's call, I can stand here as an example that God works all things for good according to His purpose.

To God be the glory!

I want to spend the rest of my life doing recovery work. You know, though, it's not really work. It's service, a service of pleasure.

This thought leads us to the last letter in give: EXAMPLE of your actions.

You all know that your actions speak louder than your words. Good intentions die unless they are executed.

In James 1:22 we are exhorted to be "doers of the word." But, in order to be of help to another, we are to "bring the Good News to others."

That's what Step 12 says. It doesn't say to bring a little good news or to bring good news only to others who are in recovery.

You have all heard the term "Sunday Christians." Let us not become just "Friday night recovery buffs."

Works, actions, not words are proof of your love for God and another person. Faith without works is like a car without gasoline. First John 3:18 (NEB) says, "My children, love must not be a matter of words or talk; it must be genuine, and show itself in action."

Giving and serving is a thermometer of your love. You *can* give without loving. That's what we sometimes do in a codependent relationship. Or we give because we feel we have to. You can give without loving, but you can't love without giving.

Wrap-up

The Lord spreads His message through the eight principles and the 12 Steps. We are the instruments for delivering the Good News. The way we live will show others our commitment to our program, to our Lord, and to them!

You have all heard the divine paradox, "You can't keep it unless you give it away!" That's Principle 8.

I would like to leave you with Luke 8:16–19 from *The Message*: "No one lights a lamp and then covers it with a washtub or shoves it under the bed. No, you set it up on a lamp stand so those who enter the room can see their way."

We're not hiding things; we're bringing everything out into the open. So be careful that you don't become misers ... generosity begets generosity. Bring the Good News with joy!

Yes

Principle 8: Yield myself to God to be used to bring this Good News to others, both by my example and by my words.

Happy are those who are persecuted because they do what God requires.

Step 12: Having had a spiritual experience as the result of these steps, we try to carry this message to others and to practice these principles in all our affairs.

Brothers, if someone is caught in a sin, you who are spiritual should restore him gently. But watch yourself, or you also may be tempted.

Galatians 6:1

Introduction

Modern technology is something else! Take an old, beat-up Diet Coke can—dirty, dented, holes in it. A few years ago, it would have been thrown in the garbage and deemed useless, of no value. Today it can be recycled, melted down, purified, and made into a new can—shiny and clean—that can be used again.

We're going to talk about recycling tonight—recycling your pain by allowing God's fire and light to shine on it, to melt down your old hurts, habits, and hang-ups so they can be used again in a positive way. They can be recycled to show others how you worked the principles and steps with Jesus' healing into the solution and how you have come through the darkness of your pain into Christ's glorious freedom and light.

Society tells us that pain is useless. In fact, people are coming to believe that *people* in pain are useless! At Celebrate Recovery, we know that pain has value, as do the people who experience it. So while the world says no, tonight we say yes!

Yes

Tonight's acrostic couldn't be any more positive! It is the word YES.

Yield myself to God

Example is what is important

Serve others as Jesus Christ did

The *Y* is Principle 8 itself: YIELD myself to God to be used to bring this Good News to others, both by my example and by my words.

To truly practice this principle, we must give God the latitude He needs to use us as He sees fit. We do that by presenting everything we have—our time, talents, and treasures—to Him. We hold loosely all that we call our own, recognizing that all of it comes from His hand. When we have yielded to Him, God can use us as His instruments to carry the message to others in word and action.

Galatians 6:1–2 (TLB) tells us: "If a Christian is overcome by some sin,... humbly help him back onto the right path, remembering that the next time it might be one of you who is in the wrong. Share each other's troubles and problems, and so obey our Lord's command."

People take your example far more seriously than they take your advice.

That leads us to the *E* in yes: EXAMPLE is what is important!

Your walk needs to match your talk. We all know that talk is cheap, because the supply always exceeds the demand.

As Pastor Rick Warren says, "If you want someone to see what Christ will do for them, let them see what Christ has done for you."

Here is a question to ask yourself when you get to this principle: Does my lifestyle reflect what I believe? In other words, does it show others the patterns of the world—selfishness, pride, and lust—or does it reflect the love, humility, and service of Jesus Christ?

"Arouse the love that comes from a pure heart, a clear conscience, and a genuine faith" (1 Timothy 1:5 GNB).

This year, we have all been blessed by some outstanding and courageous testimonies at Celebrate Recovery. I would like all those who gave their testimonies this year to stand. These people believe in Principle 8! They believe in it enough to share not only in the safety of their small groups but also with the whole recovery family. They believe in Jesus Christ enough to share their lives with others. They stood up here and shared their weaknesses and strengths with others who are suffering from similar pain, hurts, hang-ups, and habits. They gave others a piece of their heart—not a piece of their mind.

Our goal again for next year is to have two testimonies each month as we work on each step. So, if you have been in recovery for awhile and haven't shared your story as yet, get busy, write it out, and get it to me. We need to hear and you need to share your miracle in the coming year.

The last letter in yes is *S: SERVE others as Jesus Christ did.*

When you have reached Principle 8, you are ready to pick up the "Lord's towel," the one with which He washed the disciples' feet in the upper room the night before He was crucified.

Jesus said, "And since I, the Lord and Teacher, have washed your feet, you ought to wash each other's feet. I have given you an example to follow: do as I have done to you" (John 13:14–15 TLB).

You don't all have to give your testimonies to three hundred people to do service. All service ranks the same with God. You can say "y-e-s" to Principle 8 in many ways!

1. Be an accountability partner. Find someone in your small group who agrees to encourage and support you as you work through the principles. You agree to do the same for them. You hold one another accountable for working an honest program.

2. Be a sponsor. A sponsor is someone who has worked the steps. Their job is to guide a newcomer on their journey through the steps. They can give a gentle nudge when the person who they are sponsoring is procrastinating, and slow them down when they are rushing through a step. A sponsor does so by sharing their experience, strength, and hopes.

3. Become a greeter. Greeters get to Celebrate Recovery at 6:45 P.M. They welcome and provide directions for newcomers. They provide the newcomer with the important first impression of Celebrate Recovery!

4. Help with the Solid Rock Cafe. You need to arrive by 6:00 P.M. to help set up. If you can't get here early, stay a few minutes after to help clean up. You can bake a cake.

5. Help with the Bar-B-Que. We'll be starting in the spring. We need help with set-up, clean-up, and everything in between.

6. Invite someone to church. Ask someone from your secular groups or a neighbor, a friend, or a coworker!

The world is full of two kinds of people—givers and takers. The takers eat well and the givers sleep well. Be a giver. There are many, many more areas to serve! Make suggestions! Get involved!

Principle 8 comes down to this: Do what you can, with what you have, where you are.

Make your life a mission, not an intermission!

Wrap-up

The road to recovery leads to service. When you reach Principle 8 the road splits (see page 206 for a diagram). Some of you will choose to serve at Celebrate Recovery. Others will choose to serve in other areas of the church. The fact is, we need both.

We need you to share your experiences, strengths, and hopes with newcomers here on Friday nights. You do that as leaders, sponsors, and accountability partners. But the church also needs your service. As you serve outside of Celebrate Recovery, you can share with others and get them into recovery when they are ready to work on their hurts, hang-ups, and habits.

Every morning, before I get out of bed I pray this Principle 8 prayer:

> *Dear Jesus, as it would please You, bring me someone today whom I can serve.* AMEN.

Will you pray it this week?

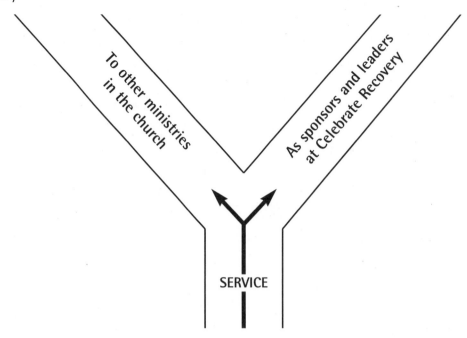

To other ministries in the church

As sponsors and leaders at Celebrate Recovery

SERVICE

PRINCIPLE 8 TESTIMONY

My name is Bob, and thanks to the power of my Lord and Savior, Jesus Christ, I have recovered from a seemingly hopeless state of mind and body commonly known as alcohol and drug addiction. I'd like to share with you how God has guided my life, led me in ways I never dreamed of, and made positive changes in my life as a result.

I came from a loving home where there was no alcoholism or abuse of any kind. I did all the normal things that kids did while I was growing up and was very involved in sports, mainly soccer.

During these years everything seemed fine, until I got into junior high, at which time I began experimenting with drugs and alcohol. I really liked the way they made me feel and I really thought it was cool at that time. I liked what it did so much that I began doing it on a regular basis. This ultimately led to harder drugs and heavier drinking. The consequence of which was a lot more problems in my life, such as being expelled from school, arguments at home, and a continuous shortage of money. I lived in a constant state of confusion because of the direction my chemical abuse was leading me.

In spite of numerous treatments at many rehab programs, which I agreed to in order to satisfy my family, I continued to live in denial of my addiction. Drugs and alcohol appeared to be my solution for a problem based on low self-esteem. After three more years of this behavior, my family could not take it any more; I had become a danger to my family at home and to those I worked with. My family finally put their foot down and decided to fire me from the family business and throw me out of the house unless I sobered up. The fear of being left with nothing caused me to try sobriety on my own and to redirect my path, but without the help of Jesus Christ I failed miserably, bringing more pain and frustration in my life. It was obvious to everyone that the path I was following was one of misery and destruction, created by my own self-will. I'd have to say that the first way God led me was to recognize my need for Him.

Next, God led me to realize that I was powerless to change the habits, hurts and hang-ups that were destroying my life. This was my first step on my road to recovery. Soon after I went to an AA meeting and met a Christian man who invited me to this church and Celebrate Recovery. This program helped me realize that meetings were not enough and that my recovery depended on my relationship with Jesus Christ. It was then that I asked Him to be my Lord and Savior and director of my life. He began to guide me away from my old path and toward His holy Word where I learned in the book of Proverbs that if I trust Him with all my heart, lean not on my own understanding, acknowledge Him in all my ways, He promises to make my path straight.

As I started to walk down my road to recovery He had planned for me, He gave me a deep desire to mend the destruction of my past through the ministry of Celebrate Recovery led by Pastor John Baker. I had a sincere hope to be of service to others who suffered as I did with addiction. His path also led me to the completion of a New Believer's Bible Study, which was necessary in order to build a solid foundation in this exciting new relationship with Christ. In addition to laying this new foundation, He also put on my heart to attend Classes 101, 201, and 301 at Saddleback. Afterward, I was baptized, became a member of the church, and attended Life Perspectives Bible Study led by Pastor Tom Holladay, Kay Warren, and Dr. Ron Rhodes. They taught me more about God's love for me and the plans He has for my future.

Following this path that He planned for me has caused my relationship with Him to grow through prayer and regular reading of His Word. God began showing me how I could make a real difference with my life by becoming a small group leader in Celebrate Recovery, where I can be of service to those who attend our meetings. Also I have become a lay pastor at our church, which provides me with even more opportunity to serve the Lord's Supper, baptize, and to help those in need. This earnest desire to serve my fellow man is a gift that only Jesus Christ could have blessed me with. He continues to bless my life by allowing me to share His love with the children in Adventure Land.

Not only has he been faithful by guiding me in my ministries, He also has been guiding me in other areas of my life such as bringing into my life a beautiful, kind, and sincere woman who loves our Lord Jesus Christ as much as or more than I do myself. As for my family and my job, instead of firing me and tossing me out of the house, they are now training me to take over the family business. Most of all, God has seen fit to use me in bringing other members of my family to a saving knowledge of Jesus Christ, and they are now active members of this church. My mother, who never gave up on me and faithfully prayed for me for ten years, is battling her fourth reoccurrence of cancer. Her faith continues to grow as God uses her to encourage others through the Caring Hearts ministry and Cancer Support Group. My sister has also been involved with the ministry for Young Adults.

Praise the Lord! All things do work together for good for those that love God and are called according to His purpose.

It has only been a year and a half since my Lord has taken me off my path of misery and destruction and placed me on the road to recovery. As for low self-esteem, it completely disappeared when I was brought into the service of a loving God who will never leave nor forsake me. He continues to make it very clear that the only life worth living is by grace alone through faith alone in Christ alone. Let Jesus Christ do the driving in your life. You won't get lost. He'll direct you through all the curves of life. Don't be afraid to trust God with your life! He promises to lead us down a path of righteousness for His name's sake—now and into eternity.

Thanks for letting me share.

The Seven Reasons We Get Stuck

Introduction

Tonight, I want to call a time-out. Let's take a week to have you discuss and evaluate where you are on your individual roads to recovery. I believe it is valuable for us all to take a breath, pause, and review our program. We need to stop for a moment and thank God as we look back on our progress and our growth. We need to make sure we are still moving forward through the principles, that we are not hung up on a particular one.

Some of you may have just begun the journey through the principles. Others are somewhere in the middle. It really doesn't matter which one you're on. Anyone can get off track and stuck.

Seven Reasons

Tonight we are going to talk about the seven reasons we get "stuck" in our recoveries!

You have not completely worked the previous principle

Perhaps, you are trying to move through the principles too quickly. Slow down! Give God time to work! Just moving forward isn't always progress. Did your brakes ever go out when you were driving down a hill? You may be going fast, but it's not progress. It's panic! Remember, this program is a process. It's not a race to see who finishes first.

Galatians 5:25 says, "Since we live by the Spirit, let us keep in step with the Spirit."

Take your time with each principle. Work it to the best of your ability. Remember, many people get lost while trying to find an easier route for the straight and narrow.

You have not completely surrendered your will and your life to the Lord

Remember, there are two parts to Principle 3. The first is to ask Jesus Christ into your heart as your Higher Power, your Lord and Savior. The second is to seek to follow His will for your life in all your decisions. Perhaps you are trusting Jesus with the "big" things, but you still think you can handle the "small" things.

Proverbs 3:5–6 (TLB) tells us, "For good judgment and common sense, . . . trust in the Lord completely; don't ever trust in yourself. In everything you do, put God first, and he will direct you and crown your efforts with success."

What part of your life are you still holding on to? What areas of your life are you withholding from God? What don't you trust Him with?

You have not accepted Jesus' work on the cross for your forgiveness

You may have forgiven others, but you think your sin is too big to be forgiven.

First John 1:9 (TLB) tells us, "If we confess our sins to him, he can be depended on to forgive us and cleanse us from every wrong." Every wrong! Not just some of our wrongs, but all of them! Believe me, your sin isn't that special, isn't that different.

"So overflowing is his kindness towards us that he took away all our sins through the blood of his Son, by whom we are saved" (Ephesians 1:7 TLB). The verse says, "all of our sins." Not some of these and some of those, but all of our sins. Period.

I think the real question here is "Have you forgiven yourself?" That's where I see most people getting stuck in their recoveries.

This is what God wants you to do with the darkness of your past: "'Come now, let us reason together,' says the Lord. 'Though your sins are like scarlet, they shall be as white as snow; though they are red as crimson, they shall be like wool'" (Isaiah 1:18).

You have not forgiven others who have harmed you

You must let go of the pain of past harm and abuse. Until you are able to release it and forgive it, it will continue to hold you as its prisoner.

It has been said that forgiveness is the key that unlocks the door of resentments and removes the handcuffs of hate. It is the power that breaks the chains of bitterness and the shackles of selfishness.

God's Word promises in 1 Peter 5:10–11(TLB): "After you have suffered a little while, our God, who is full of kindness through Christ, will give you his eternal glory. He personally will pick you up, and set you firmly in place, and make you stronger than ever."

Do you know that you may need to ask forgiveness for blaming God? Let Him off the hook for what others chose to do to you.

There is God's will, the devil's will, and your free will all at work on the earth. Remember, the harm others did to you was from their free will, not God's will.

You are afraid of the risk in making the necessary change

It may be fair to say that some people here tonight put off change and procrastinate as long as they can. There can be several reasons for delaying positive change.

You may be paralyzed by the fear of failure.

Remember, falling down doesn't make you a failure. It's staying down that makes you one. This is where your faith and trust in Jesus Christ comes into play.

You may fear intimacy because of the fear of rejection or being hurt again.

This is why it is so important to move slowly in a new relationship, taking time to seek God's will, develop realistic expectations, and establish proper boundaries.

You may resist change (growth) because of the fear of the unknown.

My life is a mess, my relationships are a mess, but at least I know what to expect. All together now—"a mess!" If you really try working the steps and principles on that hurt, hang-up, or habit, your life will change.

Some people change jobs, mates, and friends, but never think of changing themselves. What does God's Word tell us?

"Fear not, for I am with you. Do not be dismayed. . . . I will strengthen you; I will help you; I will uphold you with my victorious right hand" (Isaiah 41:10 TLB).

"We can say without any doubt or fear, 'The Lord is my Helper and I am not afraid of anything that mere man can do to me'" (Hebrews 13:6 TLB).

You are not willing to "own" your responsibility

None of us is responsible for all the things that have happened to us. But we are responsible for the way we react to them. Let me give you some examples.

In the case of abuse, in no way is the victim at fault or responsible for the abuse.

Step 8 in our sexual/physical abuse 12 Steps reads as follows:

Made a list of all persons who have harmed us and became willing to seek God's help in forgiving our perpetrators as well as forgiving ourselves. Realize that we have also harmed others and become willing to make amends to them.

My kids are not responsible for being children of an alcoholic, but they are responsible for their own actions and recovery. You need to take the responsibility for your part in a broken relationship, a damaged friendship, a distant child or parent.

"Examine me, O God, and know my mind; test me, and discover . . . if there is any evil in me and guide me in thy everlasting way" (Psalm 139:23 GNB).

We increase our ability, stability, and responsibility when we increase our accountability to God.

You have not developed an effective support team

Do you have a sponsor or an accountability partner? Do you have the phone numbers of others in your small group? Have you volunteered for a 12-Step commitment to your support group?

There are a lot of opportunities to get involved at Celebrate Recovery:

Bar-B-Que team

Solid Rock Cafe team

Bulletin stuffers

Greeters

Sponsors

Accountability Partners

Much more ...

All you have to do is ask!

"Be with wise men and become wise. Be with evil men and become evil" (Proverbs 13:20 TLB).

"Dear brothers, you have been given freedom: not freedom to do wrong, but freedom to love and serve each other" (Galatians 5:13 TLB).

"Share each other's troubles and problems, and so obey our Lord's command" (Galatians 6:2 TLB).

Remember, the roots of happiness grow deepest in the soil of service.

Wrap-up

Now you know the seven areas in which we can get bogged down, stuck in our recoveries. How do I know? Because somewhere along my own personal road to recovery, I visited them all.

Take time this week and reflect on your progress, your growth. If you are stuck, talk to your accountability partner, your sponsor, or your small group leader. Find out which of the seven reasons you are hung-up on, and together, implement a plan of action and move ahead on your journey.

Keep Celebrate Recovery's Daily Action Plan for Serenity (page 61 in Participant's Guide 4) where you can see it and review it daily.

Celebrate Recovery's Daily Action Plan for Serenity

1. Daily, continue to take an inventory. When you are wrong, promptly admit it.

2. Daily, study and pray asking God to guide you and help you apply His teaching and will in your life.

3. Daily, work and live the principles to the best of your ability, always looking for new opportunities to help and serve others—not just at your recovery meetings but in all areas of your life.

Closing Thoughts

Oh, how kind our Lord was, for he showed me how to trust him and become full of the love of Christ Jesus. How true it is, and how I long that everyone should know it, that Christ Jesus came into the world to save sinners—and I was the greatest of them all. But God had mercy on me so that Christ Jesus could use me as an example to show everyone how patient he is with even the worst sinners, so that others will realize that they, too, can have everlasting life. Glory and honor to God forever and ever. He is the King of the ages, the unseen one who never dies; he alone is God, and full of wisdom. Amen. *(1 Timothy 1:14–17 TLB)*

We have come to the end of this leader's guide, but you are now ready to begin the most exciting part—the actual stepping out and starting one of the most important and significant ministries in your church. Please feel free to use the handouts and all or any part of the lessons.

I want to pray for you and your new recovery program. Romans 12 :10–13 (NCV) tells us to "Love each other like brothers and sisters. Give each other more honor than you want for yourselves. Do not be lazy but work hard, serving the Lord with all your heart. Be joyful because you have hope. Be patient when trouble comes, and pray at all times. Share with God's people who need help. Bring strangers in need into your homes."

Please write to me or visit our website and share your progress, struggles, and prayer requests.

Write to:

John Baker
Celebrate Recovery Books
25422 Trabuco Rd. #105–151
Lake Forest, CA 92630
www.CelebrateRecovery.com

I am looking forward to learning about all the lives that will be changed and families reunited because of your decision to start a Christ-centered recovery program.

Keep coming back!

John Baker

Appendix A

Celebrate Recovery

Leadership Covenant

- I have read and agree to follow the Celebrate Recovery Leadership Manual.

- I will attend monthly Celebrate Recovery leaders' meetings.

- I will do my best to uphold Celebrate Recovery's five rules in my Small Group meetings.

- I will pray for each person in my group.

- I will pray for the unity, health, and growth of the church.

- I will squelch gossip with the truth.

- I will continue working on my personal recovery and support team.

- I will develop another person to be my coleader.

- I will follow Saddleback's Staff Standards for maintaining moral integrity.

Signed _____   _____
               Leader   Pastor

Date _____

Saddleback Staff Standards

For Maintaining Moral Integrity
Established by Pastor Rick (1986)

1. Thou shalt not visit the opposite sex alone at home.

2. Thou shalt not counsel the opposite sex alone at the office.

3. Thou shalt not counsel the opposite sex more than once without that person's mate. Refer them.

4. Thou shalt not go to lunch alone with the opposite sex.

5. Thou shalt not kiss any attender of the opposite sex or show affection that could be questioned.

6. Thou shalt not discuss detailed sexual problems with the opposite sex in counseling. Refer them.

7. Thou shalt not discuss thy marriage problems with an attender of the opposite sex.

8. Thou shalt be careful in answering cards and letters from the opposite sex.

9. Thou shalt make thy secretary thy protective ally.

10. Thou shalt pray for the integrity of other staff members.

"But among you there must not be even a hint of sexual immorality, or of any kind of impurity, or of greed, because these are improper for God's holy people." (Eph. 5:3)

Celebrate Recovery

BAR-B-QUE

FRIDAYS
6:00 to 7:00 p.m.

Bar-B-Que Dinners

- Recovery DOG — $2.00
- Serenity SAUSAGE — $3.00
- Denial BURGER — $3.00
- 12 Step CHICKEN — $3.50

Great Fellowship

- Great opportunity to share 1 to 1
- Good time to find a sponsor or accountability partner

Celebrate Recovery

at the

SOLID ROCK CAFE

EVERY FRIDAY
9:00 to 10:30 p.m. in Room 402

- *Great Fellowship*
- *Great Coffee*
- *Great Music*

Coffee donated by Haute Caffe
$1.00 donation

celebrate

My grace is enough for you ...

MY GRACE IS ENOUGH FOR YOU; FOR WHERE THERE IS WEAKNESS, MY POWER IS SHOWN MORE COMPLETELY. THEREFORE, I HAVE CHEERFULLY MADE UP MY MIND TO BE PROUD OF MY WEAKNESSES, BECAUSE THEY MEAN A DEEPER EXPERIENCE OF THE POWER OF CHRIST. I CAN EVEN ENJOY WEAKNESS, INSULTS, PRIVATIONS, PERSECUTIONS AND DIFFICULTIES FOR CHRIST'S SAKE. FOR MY VERY WEAKNESS MAKES ME STRONG IN HIM.

2 CORINTHIANS 12:9–10

Recovery

Recovery Groups

- Adult Children of the Chemically Addicted
- Codependent Men and Women in Recovery
- Chemically Dependent Men and Women in Recovery
- Eating Disorders
- Teens in Recovery – "TNT"
- Celebrate Kids 5 to 11 years old
- Women in Recovery for Sexual/Physical Abuse
- Renewal from Sexual Addiction (Men's Group)
- Welcome Home – Veterans in Recovery

Do You Have An Accountability Partner?

We encourage you to exchange telephone numbers:

Name _____   Telephone Number _____

FRIDAYS at 7:00 p.m.
For more information call 581-9100 x 167

Saddleback Church
(714) 581-5683   FAX (714) 581-7614

Mailing address: 23456 Madero, Suite 100, Mission Viejo, CA 92691
Church location: 1 Saddleback Parkway, Lake Forest, CA 92630

"Celebrate Recovery"

The purpose of Saddleback Valley Community Church's Celebrate Recovery is to fellowship and celebrate God's healing power in our lives through eight recovery principles and the Christ-centered 12 Steps. This experience allows us to be changed. We open the door by sharing our experiences, strengths, and hopes with one another. In addition, we become willing to accept God's grace in solving our life problems.

By working the steps and applying their Biblical principles, we begin to grow spiritually. We become free from our addictive, compulsive, and dysfunctional behaviors. This freedom creates peace, serenity, joy, and most importantly, a stronger personal relationship with God and others.

As we progress through the principles we discover our personal, loving, and forgiving Higher Power – Jesus Christ.

Welcome to an Amazing Spiritual Adventure

Prayer for Serenity

God, grant me the serenity
to accept the things I cannot change,
the courage to change the things I can,
and the wisdom to know the difference.
Living one day at a time,
enjoying one moment at a time;
accepting hardship as a pathway to peace;
taking, as Jesus did, this sinful world as it is;
not as I would have it;
trusting that You will make all things right
if I surrender to your will;
so that I may be reasonably happy in this life
and supremely happy with You forever in the n
AMEN
Reinhold Niebuhr

The Road to Recovery

8 Principles Based on the BEATITUDES
by Pastor Rick

R = realize I'm not God. I admit that I am powerless to control my tendency to do the wrong thing and that my life is unmanageable.

"Happy are those who know they are spiritually poor."

E = earnestly believe that God exists, that I matter to Him, and that He has the power to help me recover.

"Happy are those who mourn, for they shall be comforted."

C = consciously choose to commit all my life and will to Christ's care and control.

"Happy are the meek."

O = openly examine and confess my faults to myself, to God, and to someone I trust.

"Happy are the pure in heart."

V = voluntarily submit to every change God wants to make in my life and humbly ask Him to remove my character defects.

"Happy are those whose greatest desire is to do what God requires."

E = evaluate all my relationships. Offer forgiveness to those who have hurt me and make amends for harm I've done to others, except when to do so would harm them or others.

"Happy are the merciful." "Happy are the peacemakers."

R = reserve a daily time with God for self-examination, Bible reading, and prayer in order to know God and His will for my life and to gain the power to follow His will.

Y = yield myself to God to be used to bring this Good News to others, both by my example and by my words.

"Happy are those who are persecuted because they do what God requires."

OCTOBER 10, 1997

Songs of Celebration

There Is No One Like The Lord

There is no one,
There is no one,
There is no one like the Lord.

There is no one,
There is no one,
There is no one like the Lord.

He is mercy, He is love,
He's the happiness
The world's been dreaming of.
He's our Savior, He's our Friend,
He is holy, the beginning and the end.

© 1993 Encouraging Music
Rick Muchow

More of You

More of You in my life
More of You in my life
I need Your Word
Much more than gold
If I could have everything
It would be more of You in my life

More of You in my life
More of You in my life
I need Your love
I need Your grace
I need Your wisdom
I need more of You in my life

More of You, more of You
Knowing You is what I was made to do
Live in me, help me see
Everything You want for me to be

More of You in my life
More of You in my life
This is my prayer, this is my hope
Those who are closest to me
That they would see
More of You in my life

More of You in my life
More of You in my life
More of You in my life
More of You in my life

© 1995 Encouraging Music
Rick Warren & Rick Muchow

Day By Day

Day by day I'm growing stronger
Day by day my victory's won
As I yield my life to Jesus,
Day by day I overcome
(Repeat)

CCLI # 42373

There are days when life
Just seems too hard to face
But I know You're always near
As I trust in You my trials turn to joy
And I never need to fear

Day by day I'm growing stronger
Day by day my victory's won
As I yield my life to Jesus,
Day by day I overcome

There are days when life
Just seems too hard to face
But I know You're always near
As I trust in You my trials turn to joy
And I never need to fear

Day by day I'm growing stronger
Day by day my victory's won
As I yield my life to Jesus,
Day by day I overcome
(Repeat)

© 1990 Little Peach Music
Steve Mills, Timothy Jones & Craig Bidondo

The Power of Your Love

Lord I come to You
Let my heart be changed
Renewed, flowing from the grace
That I found in You
And Lord I've come to know
The weaknesses I see in me
Will all be stripped away
By the power of Your love

(CHORUS)
Hold me close
Let Your love surround me
Bring me near
Draw me to Your side
And as I wait I'll rise up like the eagle
And I will soar with You
Your spirit leads me on
In the power of Your love

Lord unveil my eyes
Let me see you face to face
The knowledge of Your love
As You live in me
Lord renew my mind
As Your will unfolds in my life
In living every day
By the power of Your love

(TO CHORUS)

© 1992 Nightlight Music Pty. Ltd.
Geoff Bullock

For I Know
(Jeremiah 29:11)

For I know
The plans I have for you,
Declares the Lord
Plans to prosper and not to harm you,
Plans to give you hope and a future.

© 1996 Encouraging Music
Rick Muchow

CCLI # 42373

Celebrate Recovery

SMALL GROUP MEETINGS

TUESDAY

7:30–9:00 p.m. 1st 90 Days
Chemically Dependent Men
Steps 1–3 . . . . Room 106

7:30–9:00 p.m. Men's Chemically Dependent
Step Study – Beginners . . . . Room 108

7:30–9:00 p.m. Men's Chemically Dependent
Step Study – Beginners . . . . Room 102

7:30–9:00 p.m. Men's Chemically Dependent
Step Study – Steps 4–12 . . . . Room 110

7:30–9:00 p.m. Women's Step Study . . . . Room 104

7:30–9:00 p.m. Women's 1st 90 Days . . . . Room 203

FRIDAY

7:00–9:00 p.m. . . . . CELEBRATE RECOVERY

- Adult Children of Chem. Dependent
- Chemically Dependent Men
- Chemically Dependent Women
- Codependent Men's Group
- Codependent Women's Group
- Codependent Women in a Chemically
  Dependent Relationship
- Smoking Addiction
- Sexual Addiction
- Veterans in Recovery
- Women in Recovery from
  Sexual/Physical Abuse
- Co-addicted women in a relationship
  with sexually addicted men
- Eating Disorders – Women's Group

Celebrate Recovery

Special Guest Speaker

John Townsend

Author of several books including
the bestsellers:

"The Mom Factor"
"Boundaries" and "False Assumptions"

TOPIC:

Seeking God's Will
in Your Recovery

**Friday, October 17
7:00 p.m.
in the Worship Center**

**Come for Bar-B-Que at 6:00 p.m.
Don't Miss It!**

Celebrate Recovery

Small Group Leader Guidelines

1. Keep your sharing focused on your own thoughts and feelings. Please limit your sharing to 3–5 minutes.

2. There will be no cross talk please. Cross talk is when two individuals engage in a dialogue, excluding all others. Each person is free to express feelings without interruption.

3. We are here to support one another. We will not attempt to "fix" another.

4. Anonymity and confidentiality are basic requirements. What is shared in the group stays in the group!

5. Offensive language has no place in a Christ-centered recovery group.

Celebrate Recovery

Welcome Newcomers!

The purpose of Saddleback Valley Community Church's Celebrate Recovery is to fellowship and celebrate God's healing power in our lives through the eight recovery principles found in the Beatitudes and Christ-centered 12 Steps. This experience allows us to be changed. We open the door by sharing our experiences, strengths, and hopes with one another. In addition, we become willing to accept God's grace in solving our life problems.

By working the Christ-centered steps and applying their biblical principles found in the Beatitudes, we begin to grow spiritually. We become free from our addictive, compulsive, and dysfunctional behaviors. This freedom creates peace, serenity, joy, and most importantly, a stronger personal relationship with God and others.

As we progress through the principles and the steps we discover our personal, loving, and forgiving Higher Power – Jesus Christ.

Welcome to an Amazing Spiritual Adventure!

Celebrate Recovery Small Groups CAN:

- Provide you a safe place to share your experiences, strengths, and hopes with others who are going through a Christ-centered recovery.

- Provide you with a leader who has gone through a similar hurt, hang-up, or habit, that will facilitate the group as it focuses on a particular principle each week. The leader will also keep Celebrate Recovery's "five rules."

- Provide you with the opportunity to find an accountability partner or a sponsor.

- Encourage you to attend other recovery meetings held throughout the week.

Celebrate Recovery Small Groups will NOT:

- Attempt to offer any professional clinical advice. Our leaders are not counselors. We will provide you with a list of approved counseling referrals.

- Allow its members to attempt to fix one another.

Celebrate Recovery

The Twelve Steps For Physical/Sexual Abuse

STEP ONE – We admit we are powerless over the past and as a result our lives have become unmanageable.

STEP TWO – Believe God can restore us to wholeness, and realize His power can always be trusted to bring healing and wholeness in our lives.

STEP THREE – Make a decision to turn our lives and our wills to the care of God, realizing we have not always understood His unconditional love. Choose to believe He does love us, is worth of trust, and will help us to understand Him as we seek His truth.

STEP FOUR – Make a searching and fearless moral inventory of ourselves, realizing all wrongs can be forgiven. Renounce the lie that the abuse was our fault.

STEP FIVE – Admit to God, to ourselves, and to another human being the exact nature of the wrongs in our lives. This will include those acts perpetrated against me as well as those wrongs I perpetrated against others.

STEP SIX – By accepting God's cleansing, we can renounce our shame. Now we are ready to have God remove all these character distortions and defects.

STEP SEVEN – Humbly ask Him to remove our shortcomings, including our guilt. We release our fear and submit to Him.

STEP EIGHT – Make a list of all persons who have harmed us and become willing to seek God's help in forgiving our perpetrators, as well as forgiving ourselves. Realize we've also harmed others and become willing to make amends to them.

STEP NINE – Extend forgiveness to ourselves and to others who have perpetrated against us, realizing this is an attitude of the heart, not always confrontation. Make direct amends, asking forgiveness from those people we have harmed, except when to do so would injure them or others.

STEP TEN – Continue to take personal inventory as new memories and issues surface. We continue to renounce our shame and guilt, but when we are wrong promptly admit it.

STEP ELEVEN – Continue to seek God through prayer and meditation to improve our understanding of His character. Praying for knowledge of His truth in our lives, His will for us, and for the power to carry that out.

STEP TWELVE – Having a spiritual awakening as we accept God's love and healing through these steps, we try to carry His message of hope to others. Practice these principles as new memories and issues surface claiming God's promise of restoration and wholeness.

celebrate Recovery

The Twelve Steps of the Addicted and Compulsive Person

THE "REVILED SUBSTANDARD" VERSION

1. I (not we) declared I was in complete control of my addiction/compulsion, that my life was fine and dandy – thank you very much.

2. I always knew that there was no power greater than myself, but all of you needed to be restored to sanity.

3. I made a decision to turn my will and my life over to the care of my addiction/compulsive behavior because it was the only thing that understood me.

4. I made a superficial and paranoid IMMORAL inventory of anybody but myself.

5. I admitted nothing to nobody – ever.

6. I was entirely ready to have God punish you for all your defects of character.

7. Humbly asked Him to bug somebody else.

8. Made a list of all persons who had harmed me and became willing to take revenge upon them all.

9. I took direct revenge whenever possible, especially when to do so would harm or injure them or others.

10. I continued to take other people's inventory and when they were wrong promptly told them so.

11. I sought through alcohol/drugs/relationships/food/sex/etc. to maintain unconscious contact with myself praying only for what I wanted, when I wanted it and the power to get it.

12. Having had a SPIRITUAL DEATH as a result of these steps, I tried to carry this message to other addicted/compulsive people and take as many of them as I could with me.

Celebrate Recovery

Things We ARE:

- A safe place to share
- A refuge
- A place of belonging
- A place to care for others and be cared for
- Where respect is given to each member
- Where confidentiality is highly regarded
- A place to learn
- A place to grow and become strong again
- Where you can take off your mask
- A place for healthy challenges and healthy risks
- A possible turning point in your life

Things We Are NOT:

- A place for selfish control
- Therapy
- A place for secrets
- A place to look for dating relationships
- A place to rescue or be rescued by others
- A place for perfection
- A long-term commitment
- A place to judge others
- A quick fix

celebrate Recovery

Codependency and Christian Living

On the surface, codependency messages sound like Christian teaching –

"Codependents always put others first before taking care of themselves." (Aren't Christians to put others first?)

"Codependents give themselves away." (Shouldn't Christians do the same?)

"Codependents martyr themselves." (Christianity honors its martyrs.)

Those statements have a familiar ring, don't they? Then how can we distinguish between codependency, which is unhealthy to codependents and their dependents, and mature faith, which is healthy.

Codependency says:

- I have little or no value.

- Other persons and situations have all the value.

- I must please other people regardless of the cost to my person or my values.

- I am to place myself to be used by others without protest.

- I must give myself away.

- If I claim any rights for myself, I am selfish.

Jesus taught the value of the individual. He said we are to love others equal to ourselves, not more than. A love of self forms the basis for loving others. The differences between a life of service and codependency take several forms.

Motivation differs. Does the individual give his service and himself out of free choice or because he considers himself of no value? Does he seek to "please people"? Does he act out of guilt or fear? Does he act out of a need to be needed (which means he actually uses the other person to meet his own needs; the helpee becomes an object to help the helper achieve his own goals).

- Service is to be an active choice. The person acts; codependents react.

- Codependents behavior is addictive rather than balanced. Addictions control the person instead of the person being in charge of their own life.

celebrate Recovery

Enabling

Enabling is defined as reacting to a person in such a way to shield him or her from experiencing the full impact of the harmful consequences of behavior. Enabling behavior differs from helping in that it permits or allows the person to be irresponsible.

PROTECTION from natural consequences of behavior.

KEEPING SECRETS about behavior from others in order to keep peace.

MAKING EXCUSES for the behavior. (School, friends, legal authorities, work, other family members.)

BAILING OUT of trouble. (Debts, fixing tickets, paying lawyers, providing jobs.)

BLAMING OTHERS for dependent person's behavior. (Friends, teachers, employers, family, SELF.)

SEEING THE PROBLEM AS THE RESULT OF SOMETHING ELSE. (Shyness, adolescence, loneliness, child, broken home.)

AVOIDING the chemically dependent person in order to keep peace. (Out-of-sight, out-of-mind.)

GIVING MONEY THAT IS UNDESERVED/UNEARNED.

ATTEMPTING TO CONTROL. (Planning activities, choosing friends, getting jobs.)

MAKING THREATS that have no follow-through or consistency.

TAKING CARE OF the chemically dependent person. Doing what he/she should be expected to do for themselves.

celebrate Recovery

Compliance Patterns

_____ I (not we) declared I was in complete control of my addiction/compulsion, that my life was fine and dandy – thank you very much.

_____ I feel guilty about others' feelings and behaviors.

_____ I have difficulty identifying what I am feeling.

_____ I am afraid of my anger, yet sometimes erupt in a rage.

_____ I worry how others may respond to my feelings, opinions, and behavior.

_____ I have difficulty making decisions.

_____ I am afraid of being hurt and/or rejected by others.

_____ I minimize, alter, or deny how I truly feel.

_____ I am very sensitive to how others are feeling and feel the same.

_____ I am afraid to express differing opinions or feelings.

_____ I value others' opinions and feelings more than my own.

_____ I put other people's needs and desires before mine.

_____ I am embarrassed to receive recognition and praise, or gifts.

_____ I judge everything I think, say, or do harshly, as never "good enough."

_____ I am perfectionistic.

_____ I am extremely loyal, remaining in harmful situations too long.

_____ I do not ask others to meet my needs or desires.

_____ I do not perceive myself as a lovable and worthwhile person.

_____ I compromise my own values and integrity to avoid rejection or others' anger.

Celebrate Recovery

What Is Codependence?

- My good feelings about who I am stem from being loved by you.

- My good feelings about who I am stem from receiving approval from you.

- Your struggle affects my serenity. My mental attention focuses on solving your problems or relieving your pain.

- My mental attention is focused on pleasing you.

- My mental attention is focused on protecting you.

- My self-esteem is bolstered by relieving your pain.

- My own hobbies and interests are put aside. My time is spent sharing your interests and hobbies.

- Your clothing and personal appearance are dictated by my desires as I feel you are a reflection of me.

- Your behavior is dictated by my desires as I feel you are a reflection of me.

- I am not aware of how I feel. I am aware of how you feel.

- I am not aware of what I want – I ask what you want. I am not aware – I assume.

- The dreams I have for my future are linked to you.

- My fear of rejection determines what I say or do.

- My fear of your anger determines what I say or do.

- I use giving as a way of feeling safe in our relationship.

- My social circle diminishes as I involve myself with you.

- I put my values aside in order to connect with you.

- I value your opinion and way of doing things more than my own.

- The quality of my life is in direct relation to the quality of yours.

Celebrate Recovery

Renewal From Sexual Addiction – About R.S.A.

Renewal from Sexual Addiction (RSA) is a Christ-centered recovery group for man seeking recovery from lust and compulsive sexual behaviors. The cornerstone for our recovery is the power and love of Jesus Christ. Our recovery "house" is built upon the fellowship of the group, having a safe place to share our struggles, pain, and victories, the accountability of the group, and the mutual support of group members throughout the week.

How do you know if RSA is for you? We offer the following observations of what is true for us –

We share a common experience of engaging in sexual behaviors which are demoralizing and demeaning to ourselves or another, and which we seem to be unable to stop, even in spite of the adverse consequences to our lives. We have sacrificed relationships, jobs, or our humanity, and yet we continued to engage in these damaging and compulsive sexual behaviors.

Many of us share a common history of some type of childhood abuse. We were yelled at or told we were worthless or stupid or ugly. Today we recognize these as emotional abuse. We were neglected, knocked down, or struck with objects. Today we know this to be physical abuse. Lastly, we were touched, pawed, and coerced or forced into sexual activities. Today we call this sexual abuse. Whatever abuses we suffered we learned that to survive we had to find a way to not feel the overwhelming and unbearable pain.

Instinctively we built walls around our hearts. Lust is a magical wall in that it gives the illusion of connection. So we feel safe, but we remain alone inside our prison. Unconsciously we knew that we were somehow defective, that we were different from other human beings and not normal. Sex with ourselves or with others gave us the illusion of acceptance and thus the cure to our worthlessness. We needed a constant supply of sexual activity to stay cured. To lust is to live. Lust had become the most important thing in our lives. Some of us were willing to risk and lose everything to get and keep it. Only when we came face to face with the truth that lust was a liar did we become willing to let it go. Lust promises to connect us with others and make us whole. But it never does.

Our hope:
We have accepted that we cannot control our lustful thoughts and behaviors in our own strength. We have learned that through the power of Jesus Christ we can live sober lives, one minute at a time and one day at a time. If you identify with these issues, and if you are weary from your struggle, then we invite you to fellowship with us as we daily seek the Lord's guidance on our journey of Renewal from Sexual Addiction.

Condensed and adapted from R.S.A.'s "The Problem" and "The Solution"

celebrate Recovery

New Eating Disorder Group

- Do thoughts about food occupy much of your time?

- Are you preoccupied with the desire to be thinner?

- Have you tried to diet repeatedly only to sabotage your weight loss?

- Do you exercise excessively to burn off calories?

There is a solution!

**Christ-Centered Eating Disorder
Encouragement and Accountability Recovery Group
Starts March 3, 1995
7:00 PM – Room 302
AFTER Guest Speaker Dr. Henry Cloud**

Childcare available
For more information, call 581-9100 Ext. 150

Celebrate Recovery

Eating Disorders Group

Welcome!

This recovery group's purpose is to conquer the painful effects of eating disorders. To that end we support each other as family. We seek to apply the biblical principles in the eight principles and the 12 Steps to our lives and to our relationships.

We welcome you. We cannot fix your problems, and we will not seek to run your life for you. We will accept you and love you. This is a safe place.

When we attended our first meeting, many of us were having a variety of feelings. We were relieved to find a place where people might understand our pain and despair. We were angry that we had to get help and could not manage alone this part of our lives. We felt lonely and were ashamed of the way our lives had become. We had secrets that we were reluctant to share.

Our group is not a therapy group or a study group. It is a Christ-centered recovery group. We do not give advice. We share our experience, strength, and hope with each other.

Here we learn a new way of living. We learn, at our own pace, to experience in a healthy way, intimacy and sharing with others. We learn to trust, to ask for our needs to be met, to say no when no is appropriate, to express our feelings, and to hang around when all we want to do is run. Here no one shames us for what we have done or are still doing. Here we have a safe harbor within which to heal, and for that we are grateful. The only requirement for membership in our group is a desire to change our unhealthy eating behaviors.

Those of us who have experienced life change through the program offer this challenge to you: This program works as we complete the work with the help and supervision of a sponsor or accountability partner. If you do not have a sponsor or accountability partner, we encourage you to enlist one, complete the written work in the Celebrate Recovery participant's guides, and share your work with your sponsor or accountability partner.

We are happy your are here. We encourage you to take one day at a time and keep coming back. It works.

celebrate Recovery

"Welcome Home"

Veterans In Recovery From Post Traumatic Stress Disorder

Major Symptoms of Post-Traumatic Stress Disorder (PTSD)

There are a number of primary PTSD responses we (talking about Vets) exhibit as a result of our experiences in Southeast Asia and back in the U.S. (or Canada). Psychologists and psychiatrists working with the Disabled American Veterans Outreach Program compiled the list that follows. Most Vietnam Veterans show only a few of these responses. The major PTSD responses are:

- Depression
- Cynicism and distrust of government and authority
- Anger
- Alienation
- Sleep disturbances
- Concern with humanistic values overlaid by hedonism
- Tendency to react under stress with survival tactics
- Psychic or emotional numbing
- Negative self-image
- Memory impairment
- Emotional constriction
- Hypersensitivity to justice
- Loss of interest in work or activities
- Problems with intimate relationships
- Survivor guilt
- Difficulty with authority figures
- Hyper-alertness
- Avoidance of activities that arouse memories of traumas in war zone
- Emotional distance from children, wife, and others
- Suicidal feelings and thoughts
- Flashbacks of Vietnam
- Fantasies of retaliation and destruction
- Self-deceiving and self-punishing patterns of behavior, such as an inability to talk about war experiences, fear of losing others and tendency of fits of rage

A few of these delayed stress responses may sound familiar to you and the people closest to you. But you and they may even deny these reactions when they appear.

celebrate Recovery

Recovering With Your Kids
Larry Hamilton, M.A., M.F.C.C.

6 Week Workshop FOR PARENTS ONLY
Mondays — 7–9 p.m. — Room 210

May 8   Turning Anger Into Boundaries, Limits and Definitions

May 15   Turning Guilt Into Confession, Forgiveness, and Direction

May 22   Turning Helplessness and Control Into Reality Checks

June 5   Turning Fear Into Security

June 12 Turning Feelings of Abandonment Into Confrontation and Honesty

June 19 Turning Feelings of Worthlessness and of Being Unlovable Into Acceptance and Love

celebrate Recovery

Co-Addicted Women in a Relationship with Sexually Addicted Men — COSA

What sexual addiction is and what causes it, is mostly unknown to many people. In this group we use the 8 Principles and the 12 Steps, so co-addicts can confront their own denial and behavior while gaining insight and understanding of their spouse's addiction.

Co-addicts may share the following experiences:

• Having a spouse who has continually called "900" sex numbers

• Having a spouse who is currently having or has had an affair

• They, themselves, are having an affair

• Issues dealing with molestation and abuse from spouse

• Their spouse having homosexual affairs

• Their spouse watching adult sex videos and buying pornography (magazines)

• Their spouse having sex with prostitutes

• Their spouse's obsession with sex to the point of self-injury

Through a Christ-centered recovery group, the co-addict can achieve the following:

1. Allow the co-addict to hear the faulty beliefs and struggles of other co-addicts.

2. Learn healthy, Christian values for family roles and rules.

3. Gain information about healthy sexuality and relationships.

4. Break through denial and other family patterns.

5. Encouragement from the group to find peace, strength, and grace through a personal relationship with Jesus Christ.

6. Build healthy relationships by finding love and acceptance in a "safe" place to share.

celebrate Recovery

Men in Recovery from Physical/Sexual Abuse

This is a Christ-centered recovery group for men in recovery from past physical and/or sexual abuse. One of the keys to success in recovery programs is the coming together of people with similar backgrounds who also have common goals and objectives. Our common background is a history of abuse, and our goal is to enter into or maintain recovery. Recovery for us is a twofold issue. We need healing from the traumas done to us at some time in our past; we also need healing from the influence these past experiences continue to have on our present lives.

For the newcomer, the program can be a place to recognize and identify core issues resulting from past abuse. The newcomer can receive validation and understanding, and as he practices the principles and steps among other Christian men, he can also gain knowledge that will help him choose appropriate actions in response to his life's circumstances.

For the "old-timers," those men with the same issues but who have already begun the road to recovery, this recovery group can provide a place in which to continue their recovery process.

One of our objectives is to provide a supportive and safe environment. The leader alone cannot assure that, it has to be a group effort. We respect and acknowledge each man's right to be where he needs to be on his own road to recovery. We acknowledge the sensitivity we need to have for each member of this group. Therefore, we have a few reminders that are not meant to offend but to ensure the safety and anonymity of each man present. "What you hear here, let it stay here."

As with any other Christ-centered recovery group, we believe that by our participation through active listening, sharing, and application of the steps and principles to our lives, the Holy Spirit will guide us to further understanding, healing, and wholeness.

We are not here to lecture, preach, fix, or provide therapy. We are here to tell our story. We come together to share in our weakness, for it is in our weakness that we gain strength. Ecclesiastes 4:9-12 says, "Two are better than one, because they have a good return for their work: If one falls down, his friend can help him up. But pity the man who falls and has no one to help him up! Also, if two lie down together, they will keep warm. But how can one keep warm alone? Though one may be overpowered, two can defend themselves. A cord of three strands is not quickly broken."

Accountabilty is another advantage in coming together as a group. We can look to others to honestly let us know how we are doing in our recovery. "Old-timers" or sponsors can help us see where we may be stuck or provide us with a safe "sounding board" so that we can hear ourselves.

Developing a support system is integral to the program. We find we are not alone. Others share similar stories. Support can be expanded to include phone calls with other willing members of the group. Support could also include seeking out a sponsor for added encouragement.

An important advantage is the prayer support. We can join together in prayer against any of Satan's strongholds that may be keeping us from maturing as Christians or limiting our recovery.

When we come together we share spiritual gifts.

One last advantage is that together we multiply the witness of Christ. We are not an accident. God created us to reflect the grace and love of Jesus Christ as we move through our recoveries.

Celebrate Recovery

Women in Recovery from Physical/Sexual Abuse

This is a Christ-centered recovery group for women in recovery from past physical and/or sexual abuse. One of the keys to success in recovery programs is the coming together of people with similar backgrounds who also have common goals and objectives. Our common background is a history of abuse, and our goal is to enter into or maintain recovery. Recovery for us is a twofold issue. We need healing from the traumas done to us at some time in our past; we also need healing from the influence these past experiences continue to have on our present lives.

For the newcomer, the program can be a place to recognize and identify core issues resulting from past abuse. The newcomer can receive validation, understanding, and knowledge of appropriate action to take by practicing the principles and steps among other Christian women.

For the "old-timers," those women with the same issues but who have already begun the road to recovery, this recovery group can provide a place in which to continue their recovery process.

One of our objectives is to provide a supportive and safe environment. The leader alone cannot assure that, it has to be a group effort. We respect and acknowledge each woman's right to be where she needs to be on her own road to recovery. We acknowledge the sensitivity we need to have for each member of this group. Therefore, we have a few reminders that are not meant to offend but to ensure the safety and anonymity of each woman present. "What you hear here, let it stay here."

As with any other Christ-centered recovery group, we believe that by our participation through active listening, sharing, and application of the steps and principles to our lives, the Holy Spirit will guide us to further understanding, healing, and wholeness.

We are not here to lecture, preach, fix, or provide therapy. We are here to tell our story. We come together to share in our weakness, for it is in our weakness that we gain strength. Ecclesiastes 4:9-12 says, "Two are better than one, because they have a good return for their work: If one falls down, his friend can help him up. But pity the man who falls and has no one to help him up! Also, if two lie down together, they will keep warm. But how can one keep warm alone? Though one may be overpowered, two can defend themselves. A cord of three strands is not quickly broken."

Accountabilty is another advantage in coming together as a group. We can look to others to honestly let us know how we are doing in our recovery. "Old-timers" or sponsors can help us see where we may be stuck or provide us with a safe "sounding board" so that we can hear ourselves.

Another advantage is the sharing of encouragement. The center of the word encouragement is courage. Sometimes we need others around us who have been there to give us courage to be where we are or to take action.

Developing a support system is integral to the program. We find we are not alone. Others share similar stories. Support can be expanded to include phone calls with other willing members of the group. Support could also include seeking out a sponsor for added encouragement.

An important advantage is the prayer support. We can join together in prayer against any of Satan's strongholds that may be keeping us from maturing as Christians or limiting our recovery.

When we come together we share spiritual gifts.

One last advantage is that together we multiply the witness of Christ. We are not an accident. God created us to reflect the grace and love of Jesus Christ as we move through our recoveries.